Corporate Design

Corporate Design
GRAPHIC IDENTITY SYSTEMS

Joseph W. Bereswill

PBC INTERNATIONAL, INC. ▪ New York

DISTRIBUTOR TO THE BOOK TRADE IN THE UNITED STATES:
Rizzoli International Publications, Inc.
597 Fifth Avenue
New York, NY 10017

DISTRIBUTOR TO THE ART TRADE IN THE UNITED STATES:
Letraset USA
40 Eisenhower Drive
Paramus, NJ 07653

DISTRIBUTOR IN CANADA:
Letraset Canada Limited
555 Alden Road
Markham, Ontario L3R 3L5, Canada

DISTRIBUTED THROUGHOUT THE REST OF THE WORLD BY:
Hearst Books International
105 Madison Avenue
New York, NY 10016

Copyright © 1987 by PBC INTERNATIONAL, INC.
All rights reserved. No part of this book may be reproduced
in any form whatsoever without written permission of the
copyright owner, PBC INTERNATIONAL, INC., One School Street,
Glen Cove, NY 11542.

Library of Congress Cataloging-in-Publication Data
Corporate Design.
1. Packaging — Design and construction.   I. ID
(New York, N.Y.)
TS195.2.C66 1987   688.8   87-13601
ISBN 0-86636-018-2

Color separation, printing, and binding by
Toppan Printing Co. (H.K.) Ltd. Hong Kong
Typesetting by Vera-Reyes, Inc.

Printed in Hong Kong
10 9 8 7 6 5 4 3 2 1

Publisher	**Herb Taylor**
Project Director	**Cora Sibal Taylor**
Executive Editor	**Virginia Christensen**
Editor	**Wanda P. Jankowski**
Art Director	**Richard Liu**
Production Manager	**Kevin Clark**

CONTENTS

Introduction to
Corporate Identity Graphics 8

OIL REFINING 16
Quaker State Corporation 18
Q8 — Kuwait Petroleum International 34

INSURANCE 50
Prudential Corporation 52

UNIVERSITIES 66
PennState 68
Aston University 78

GLASS MANUFACTURING 92
Pilkington 94

PRINTING 116
Gavin Martin 118

HEALTH CARE 128
Mount Carmel Health 130

Appendix 154
Indexes 156

Introduction to Corporate Identity Graphics

Today's business climate, with its increasing global economic, social, and political pressures, is causing many corporations and other business organizations to change how and, often, where they do business. As these organizations explore new markets and arenas in which to grow and prosper, many are coming face to face with an identity crisis. For some companies, this crisis is not new. For others, particularly those with a history of public acceptance and market presence, it may be unexpected.

Coping with a Corporate Identity Crisis

To meet this crisis head-on, companies are changing their names, changing the symbols of their businesses, attempting to change — which often means, clarifying — their identities, and altering their industrial packaging and design.

In the world of identity programs, the most noticeable and prevalent action being taken on an international scale by business and industry has been name changing. Organizations across North America and abroad are implementing name change programs in unprecedented numbers.

In 1986, in just the U.S. alone, 1,382 firms changed names according to a yearly corporate identity survey conducted by the business marketing communications and design consulting firm of Anspach Grossman Portugal, Inc. (AGP). Of all the industry segments examined in the 1986 AGP survey, the largest percentile increase in name changing among separate groups occurred in the communications industry, which reported a jump of 245%. In 1986, 100 such firms changed their names, while only 29 name changes were recorded a year earlier. The communications companies in the survey included press, broadcasting, and cable TV organizations. Examples of some well-known name changes in this industry category included

Capital Cities/ABC, U.S. Telecom to U.S. Sprint Communications, and the dropping of "Newspapers" from the Knight-Ridder name.

The American banking industry, primarily because of stiff intramural competition brought about by government deregulation, has experienced consecutive years of accelerated name changes through the 1980s. As a result, this single industry segment traditionally has been the name change leader in AGP's yearly identity survey. However, in the 1986 study, banking took a back seat to the U.S. general manufacturing and industrial business sector, which registered a 60% increase over the year before, or 346 changes. Name changes among banks declined by 6% in the one-year period.

The AGP survey also showed that on a regional basis, New York continued to be the leading location of firms with name changes in 1986, with 133, or almost 10% of the total. The states of California, with 85 name changes, and Pennsylvania, with 76 recorded changes, placed second and third respectively. This contrasts sharply with the 1985 survey results, which showed the states of Texas and New Jersey ranking second and third in the AGP study.

If anything, the surveys show that corporate name changing has become an almost daily occurrence in our society and a trend that is likely to continue well into the future. But it is important to note that in line with the challenge to select a proper name is the challenge to redefine an organization's culture, both internally and with its various external publics, and to select appropriate graphic symbols, color schemes, and packaging and graphic design that reflect the new shape and direction of the firm.

Using Corporate Identity Specialists

For graphic redesign, which this book essentially is about, most companies historically have hired the services of professional, external consultants. Indeed, since the earliest days of the nineteenth century industrial revolution in the United States, business leaders have sought the help of persons outside their organization to assist in the creative design and packaging of boxes, wrappers, and labels to promote their names and reinforce consumer awareness, as well as for signage and logos to assist in establishing a corporate identity. Today, image and corporate identity consultants form a separate and respected profession of their own.

In this era of litigation, no responsible firm would knowingly use a new name, logo, or package design without consulting a legal expert who specializes in researching the legality of adopting such items. Once an organization chooses a name, it quickly copyrights it and, if a symbol is to be used, registers the graphic with the U.S. Patent and Trademark Office.

In addition to the legal profession, corporate identity design consultants often work hand-in-hand with external public relations firms. The latter help to ensure the overall success of a corporate identity program by working with company management to determine whether the program is in line with the firm's goals and policies and to formulate an effective communications program for reaching the company's many audiences.

Other external consultants that may be brought in to assist with identity programs include architects and interior designers, color experts, packaging designers, trademark specialists, language experts (to avoid embarrassments such as the one that occurred when General Motors introduced the Chevy Nova in Mexico and quickly learned that "no va" in Spanish means "doesn't go"), psychologists, and others.

Case Studies in Corporate Identity Design

Corporate Design provides the reader with an opportunity to examine how design professionals created identity design programs for eight organizations with different histories, structures, and cultures. Included here are a domestic oil refining corporation, an international petroleum company, a European life insurance firm, two universities — one in the U.S. and the other in the United Kingdom, a European industrial conglomerate, a major color printing concern, and a large Midwest-based health care center.

Each of these establishments had separate and distinct identity concerns that ranged from overcoming an image problem created by a name change, to recreating a company image so that it would represent all of the company's core businesses, including those recently acquired. In the case of the domestic oil company, Quaker State Corporation, the goal of its corporate identification program was to provide even conformity and uniformity among all of its corporate and subsidiary products, services, and signage.

The unique combination of organizations in this book, which includes both U.S.-based and foreign-based institutions, illustrates how the issue of corporate identity crosses both industrial and geographic borders. The need to plan and execute a carefully defined identity program as part of an overall communications and image policy is just as important to the success of doing business in the Middle East as it is on Main Street U.S.A.

How Corporate Design Contributes to Business Success

Perhaps the most important function of industrial packaging and design systems is to create strong consumer recognition and awareness. History has shown that once an organization has committed itself to producing quality products and making the public aware of its brand items, consumers tend to return to that same brand time and again. One of the classic textbook examples of brand acceptance by consumers occurred in the mid-nineteenth century with Proctor & Gamble. At the time, P&G manufactured candles in Cincinnati, Ohio, and distributed them to storeowners in other cities along the Ohio and Mississippi rivers. Many other businesses also made candles and shipped them throughout the area. But it was not until dockworkers started branding P&G's crates with a star that the company realized that storeowners all along the river recognized the P&G star as a mark of quality. Storeowners would not accept shipments of candles that were not marked with the branded star. P&G quickly capitalized on this marketing tool by refining the mark and applying it to other consumer products that the company produced and distributed.

The same basic identity program concepts that were pioneered more than one hundred years ago have evolved, through a series of changes, into the more sophisticated concepts used today. The basic goals — to be seen by the public and to be remembered — remain the same; however, modern-day identity programs must meet additional objectives, such as reflecting the organization's image and overall culture.

At a time in our history when government regulation, worldwide competition, global economic instability, employee morale, consumer rights, and investor awareness are key business issues, successful corporate identity programs can provide the extra thin margin of success that increasingly is being needed to separate the leader from the rest of the pack.

When two large manufacturing companies make similar products, have similar advertising budgets, and offer similar product marketing support services for their distributors, it is most often a successful corporate identity program that separates number one from number two. In other words, the company which is best recognized and remembered by consumers usually emerges as the leader.

When the competition for business success is carried into the financial arena, the stakes can become much higher. A key reason is that the future growth potential of a business depends, in large part, on the firm's ability to raise money. Since the value that the financial community and investors place on the firm's securities directly affects the company's ability to raise capital, it is imperative that companies help keep their stock prices stable by creating a favorable image that instills investor confidence.

Corporate image, identity, and reputation all are important facets of any investor relations program. Of course, the corporate balance sheet is still the main road map used by security analysts, sophisticated general investors, and large institutional investors in analyzing a firm's path to success. But when Wall Street is confronted with a number of companies with similar product lines, good management structures, and similar financial statements, the deciding factor in choosing which company to invest in can be its corporate identity and name recognition and how the individual feels about the firm.

Using a Corporate Identity Program to Motivate Employees

Today's businesses also recognize that financial success hinges, to a great degree, on the abilities and motivation of its employees. History has shown that corporate identity programs can go a long way towards motivating workers and helping to avoid downcycles in employee productivity. In an economy which has, to a large degree, changed from a manufacturing economy to a high-technology, service-oriented economy, employee loyalty has ebbed to an all-time low. When translated into dollars and cents, lack of loyalty means increased absenteeism for illness and personal reasons, less time spent actually working on the job, less output, and a high rate of personnel turnover.

Conversely, employees who feel good about the company they work for and are proud to be a part of the organization feel like they "belong." They generally want to work harder on their own, take less time off from work, and want to influence their families, friends, and neighbors to buy the company's products or services. They can influence the news media's perception about the business and have a positive impact on the price of a company's stock by encouraging investment in the firm they work for.

In this day of hostile corporate takeovers, many organizations that had taken the time to foster a strong identity program with employees and foster goodwill among workers found that they could count on this important following when trying to prevent the company from falling into the wrong hands.

With this in mind, companies increasingly are involving their employees in the design and selection process as a first step in developing a name change and identity program. The internal newsletters and newspapers of a company are generally used as the primary communications vehicle to encourage all employees to participate in the process by submitting ideas and suggestions for the image and identity program. Once a new name and corporate logo are chosen, workers are generally invited to the unveiling ceremony. Corporate apparel, such as neckties, scarves, and hats, is usually distributed throughout the company and items showing the new identity often become a status symbol within the organization.

Corporate Identity in an Era of Mergers and Acquisitions

Just as the back-to-back recessions of the late 1970s resulted in massive corporate restructuring across North America and abroad, the 1980s will go down in worldwide business annals as the era of mergers and acquisitions. Interestingly, both eras saw the same end product — a change in the shape of the business organization.

The end result of corporate restructuring, through the spinning-off, or divesting, of unnecessary assets, generally is an organization much smaller in size. Mergers and acquisitions usually have the reverse effect. The two companies become a single, much larger, unit. Mergermania, therefore, is the primary reason for the current, unparallelled activity in corporate name changing.

Other Reasons for Changing a Corporation's Identity

There are reasons other than mergers and acquisitions for changing a corporation's identity, among them leveraged buyouts, installation of a new management team, moving of corporate headquarters to another location, turmoil in the international political arena, a sharp change in the makeup of a company's core businesses and traditional markets, as well as the anniversary of either a company's founding or the introduction of one of its well-known product lines.

The eight organizations highlighted in this book all faced similar identity challenges and developed varying communications solutions. These are described from the perspective of the external design consulting firms and are illustrated in full-color photographs of conceptual designs, color schemes, identity manuals, completed logos, letterheads, business cards, signage, printed matter, and numerous other items.

This book is written for modern corporate design professionals from the view of a professional corporate communicator with extensive experience in the research, design, and implementation of strategic communications and identity systems. The author is appreciative to the consultants and organizations whose names appear in this text and without whose cooperation this book would not exist.

Another frequently occurring reason for such a change has to do with problems generated by an organization's logo, name, or symbol. These could arise from a negative connotation derived from the logo or trademark itself, or from a particularly bad or dangerous product that the graphic may be associated with. Also, problems often surface when a competitor devises a similar logo, name, or symbol, or when similar graphics and designs are used on different products and services by other businesses.

When senior management decides to initiate a change in the corporation's identity, the major challenge is to define the program's goals and objectives. These could include improving the corporate structure, trying to separate the present company from its past, distinguishing a company from its business peers and competitors, trying to change the perception of an organization held by the firm's various publics such as Wall Street, consumers, and employees, and establishing a new identity for a new organization.

OIL REFINING

24 QUAKER STATE CORPORATION

Selection of Quaker State Motor Oils in one-quart plastic bottles and a five-quart plastic jug

QUAKER STATE CORPORATION 25

Application of corporate identification guidelines to Product-Sales Information Bulletins and envelope stuffers

Stadium cushion, ice bucket, and cooler with new corporate logo applied

Sales literature

QUAKER STATE CORPORATION   27

Quaker State all-purpose spray chemicals

Quaker State hand cleaners presented on truck decal

Sample of consumer print advertising

Point-of-sale poster, banner, and envelope stuffer

Quaker State sales support programs

Quaker State automotive chemicals

Quaker State lubricants and greases in a variety of package sizes

Modification of corporate design accommodating additional graphic elements

Example of retail point-of-sale literature

Quaker State customized alphabet

32 QUAKER STATE CORPORATION

Sales aids

Selection of Quaker State coating products

QUAKER STATE CORPORATION   33

Quaker State necktie

Ball cap, golf ball, and tee-pack from Quaker State selection of sales aids

Sample Quaker State trade advertising

Q8—Kuwait Petroleum International

Q8 — Kuwait Petroleum International

Headquarters:	London, England (European headquarters)
Business:	Petroleum and lubricant refining and marketing
Organization:	Subsidiary of Kuwait Petroleum, one of the world's largest oil producers, branches throughout Europe
Design:	Wolff Olins
Functions of Design Program:	Consistency of corporate identity in stationery, signage, vehicles, and the gas station/retail network design (architectural and interior)

Kuwait Petroleum International was the first OPEC producer to create a new gasoline brand and establish a retail chain. Wolff Olins advised on name, identity, and market position. The name "Q8" is memorable and applicable throughout the world, and makes an implicit link with Kuwait. The sail imagery evokes a coastal people and suits a brand concept that links travel, efficiency, and enjoyment in a way that is free of limiting associations with any particular group, age, country, or class. The stations themselves establish the Q8 identity through graphic, retail, and environmental design, which is applied in areas ranging from lighting to staff training.

Brand mark on dark background

Brand mark on light background

38 Q8 — Kuwait Petroleum International

Exterior of newly built filling station

Forecourt of new filling station

Q8 — KUWAIT PETROLEUM INTERNATIONAL

Pole sign: grades and prices

Pole sign: diesel

Q8 — KUWAIT PETROLEUM INTERNATIONAL

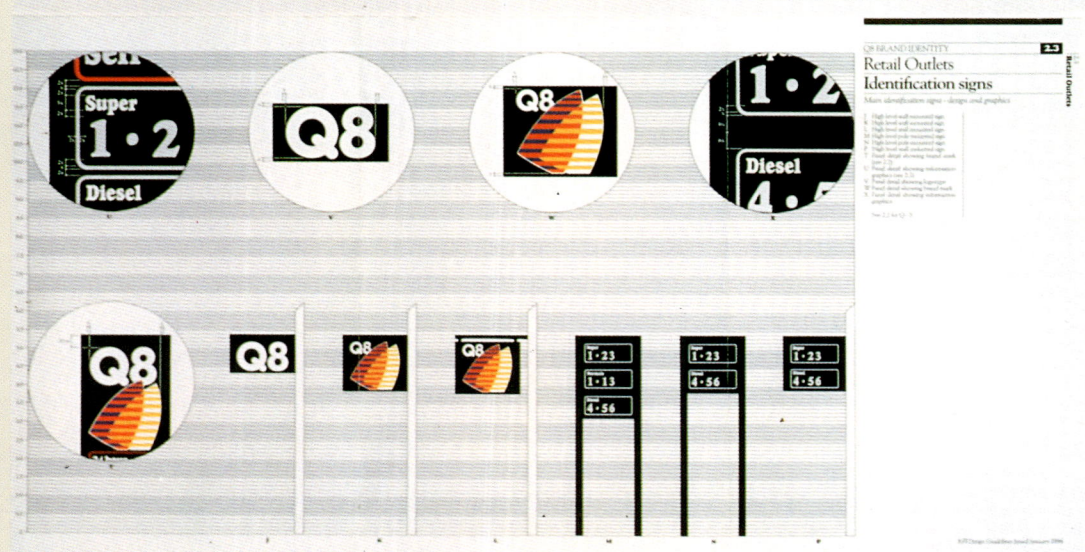

Spread from identity manual — retail units identification signs

Fascia signage detailing

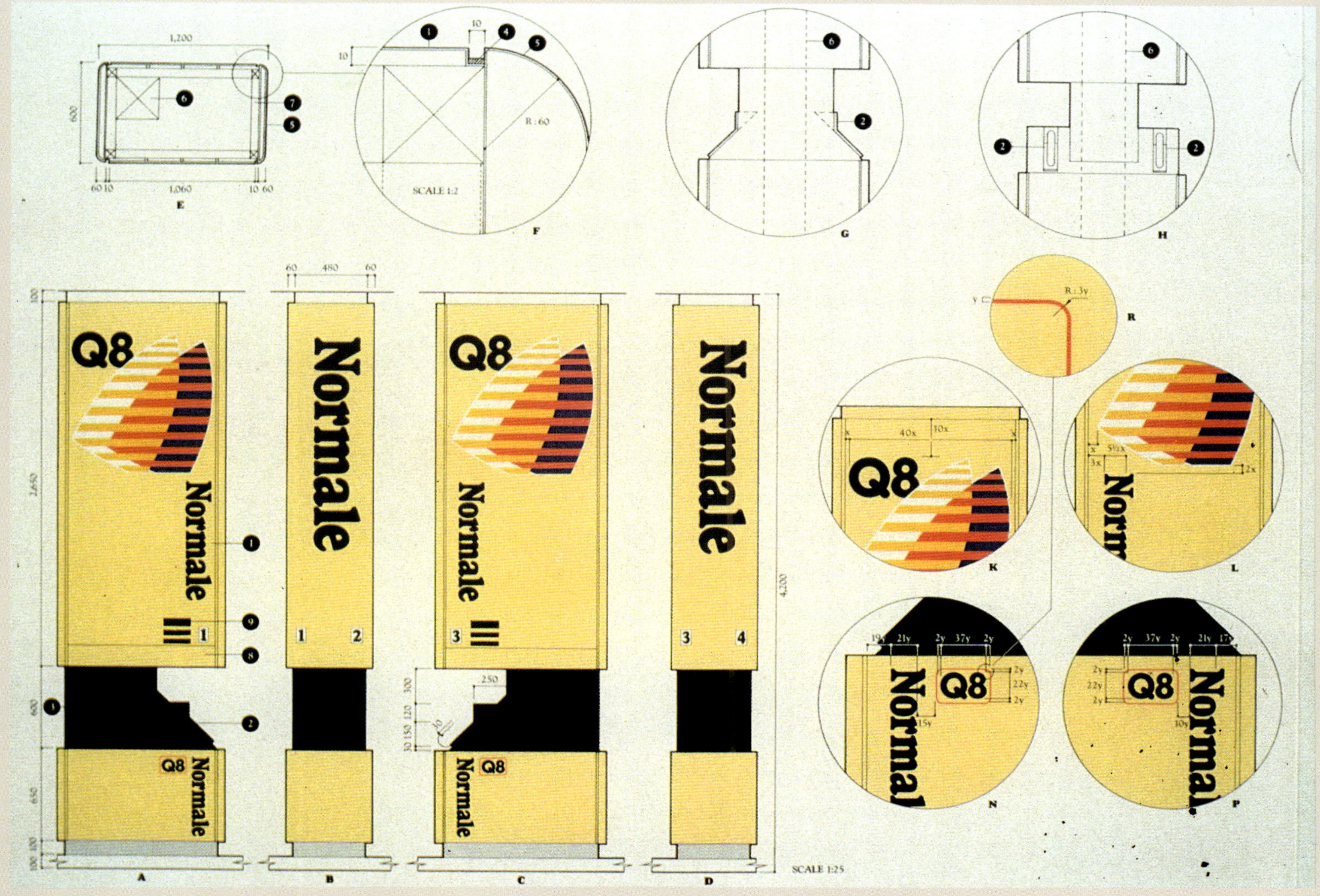

Q8 — Kuwait Petroleum International   43

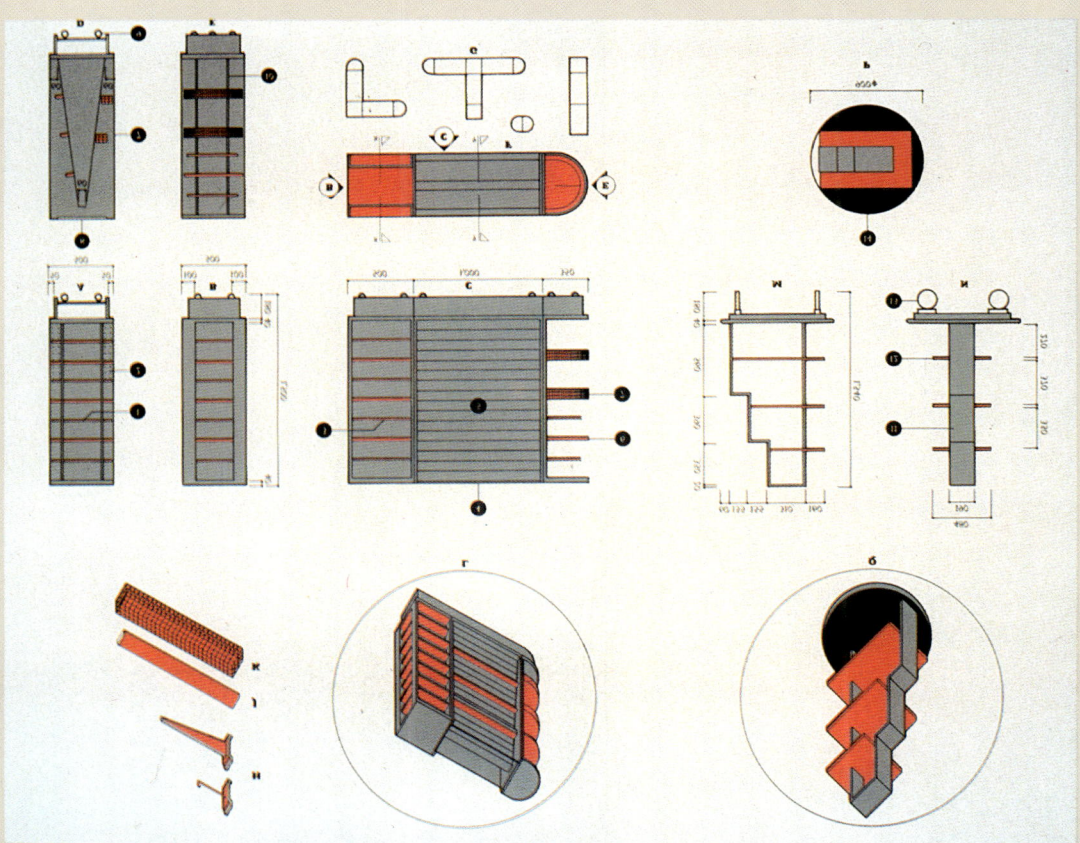

Details from identity manual — pump columns

Details from identity manual — free standing interior shop fittings

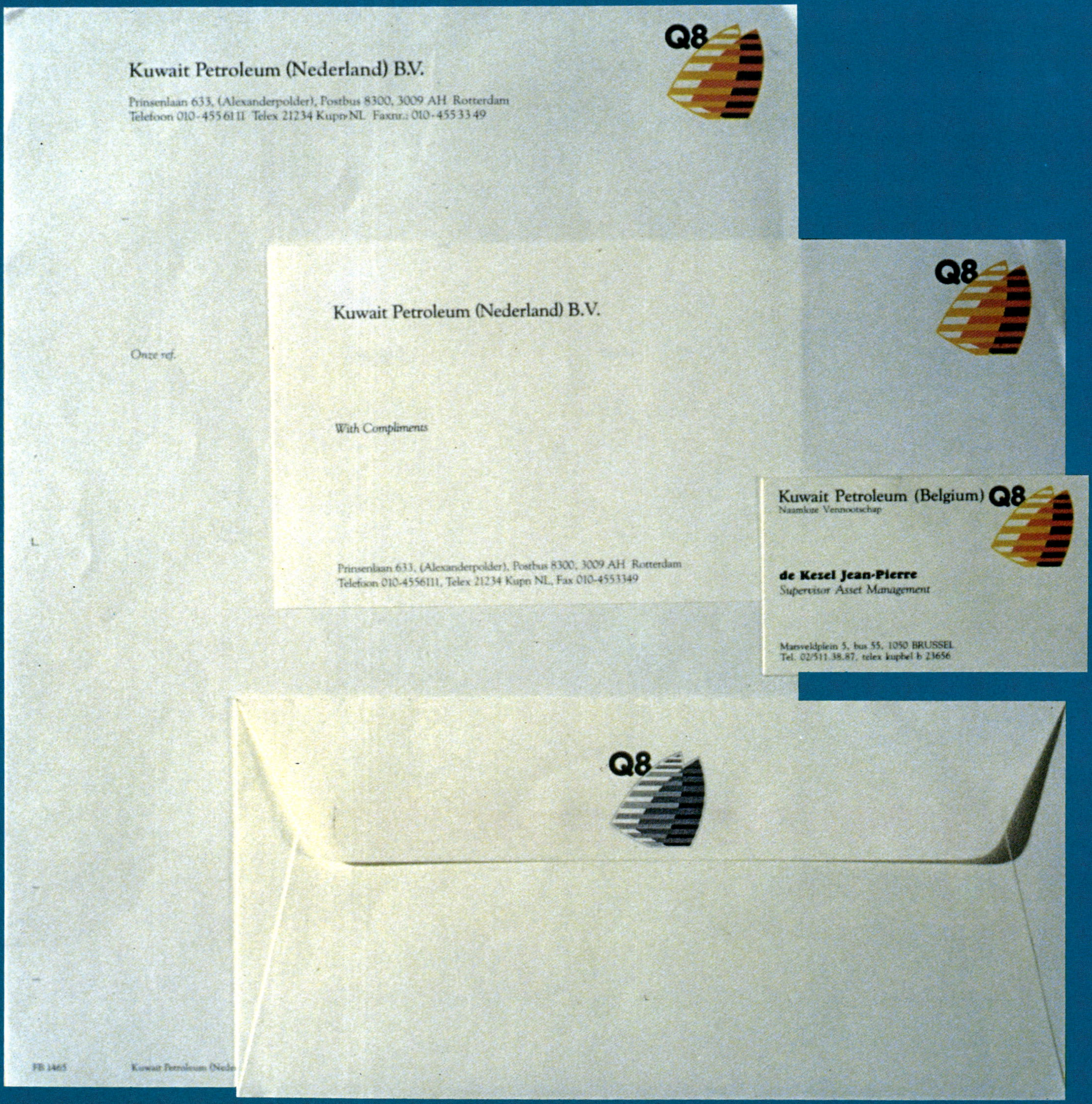

44   Q8 — Kuwait Petroleum International

Stationery

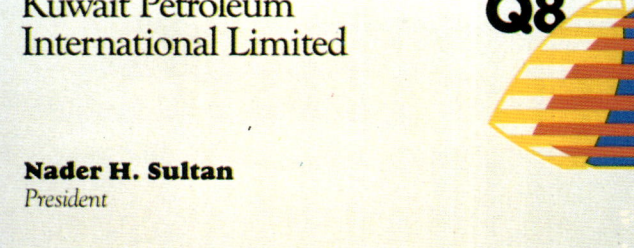

Business card

Q8 — Kuwait Petroleum International   45

In-house journal announcing launch of new identity

Forms — delivery note and invoice

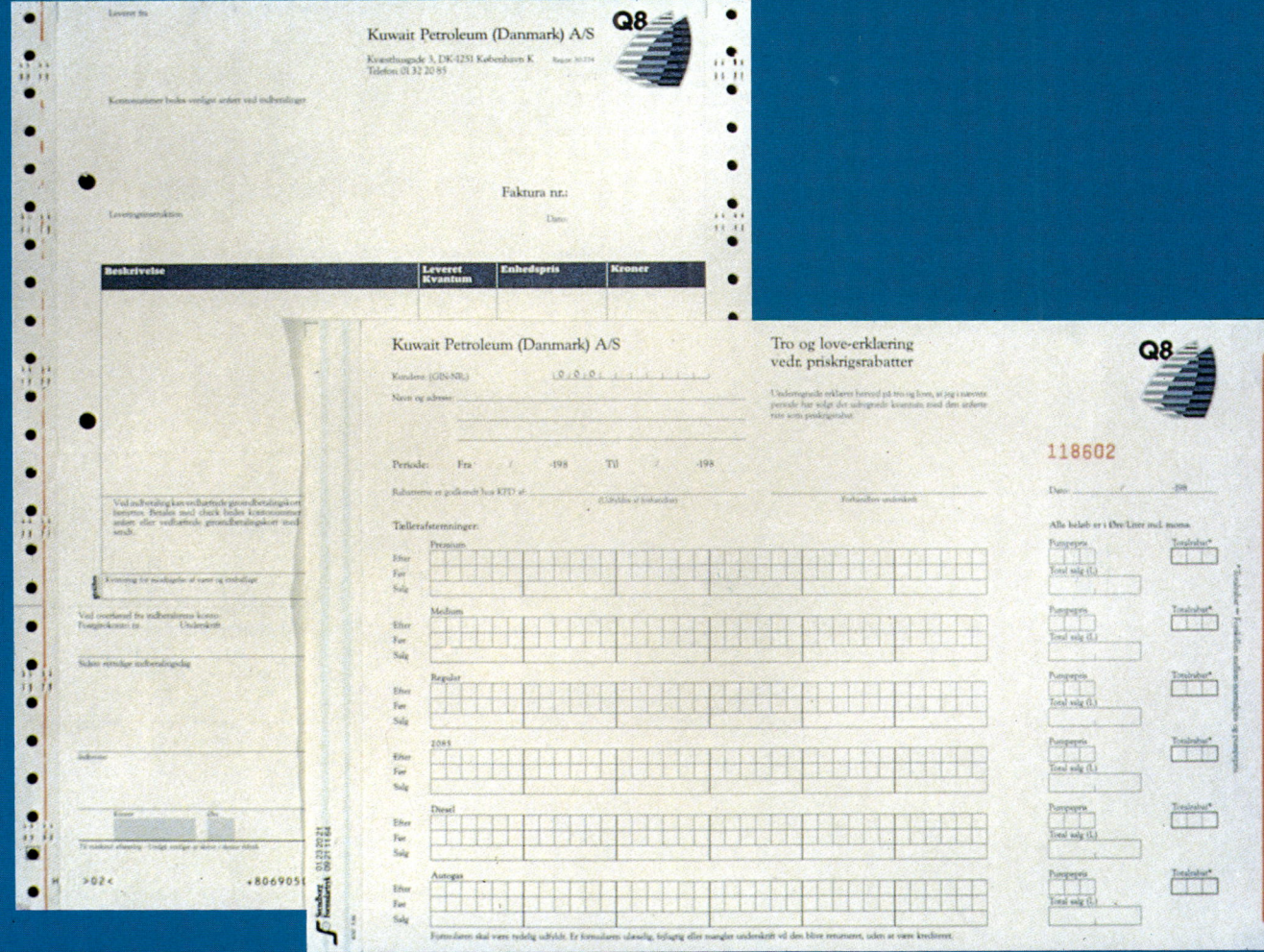

Covered pump area and Club Q8 shop

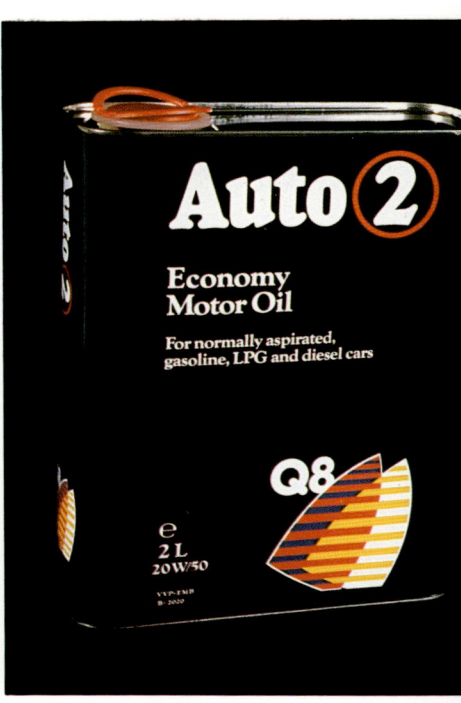
Economy Motor Oil container

Lubricant pack

Pump column, full height from ground level to canopy, housing pump units

Cold weather uniform

48 Q8 — Kuwait Petroleum International

Pump (detail)

Brand mark on glass

Aircraft re-fueling tanker

Q8 — Kuwait Petroleum International

Storage tank

INSURANCE

Prudential Corporation

HEADQUARTERS:	London, England
BUSINESS:	Financial services
ORGANIZATION:	Manages assets of over $20,000,000,000, 8 million customers holding 20 million policies, branches in 32 countries, 30,000 employees worldwide
DESIGN:	Wolff Olins
FUNCTIONS OF DESIGN PROGRAM:	Consistency of corporate identity, including guidelines for stationery, publications, advertising, signage, and building or office interiors

In Britain, the Prudential means life assurance. The group's diversity is masked by the use of several names and visual identities. Wolff Olins argues that the qualities the Prudential stands for — security, strength, prudent management — are relevant and attractive in all of its markets, and the name will now be used throughout.

The new corporate identity also draws on the power of female imagery, by reviving the company's link with Prudence, one of the platonic virtues. The classical elements of the mirror and the snake are incorporated in entirely modern imagery. The identity combines the twin strengths of the company's name and visual heritage. In the financial world, prudence is a core virtue.

PRUDENTIAL CORPORATION 55

Prudence, mirror and snake elements form logo emblazoned on flags

56   PRUDENTIAL CORPORATION

Brass nameplate

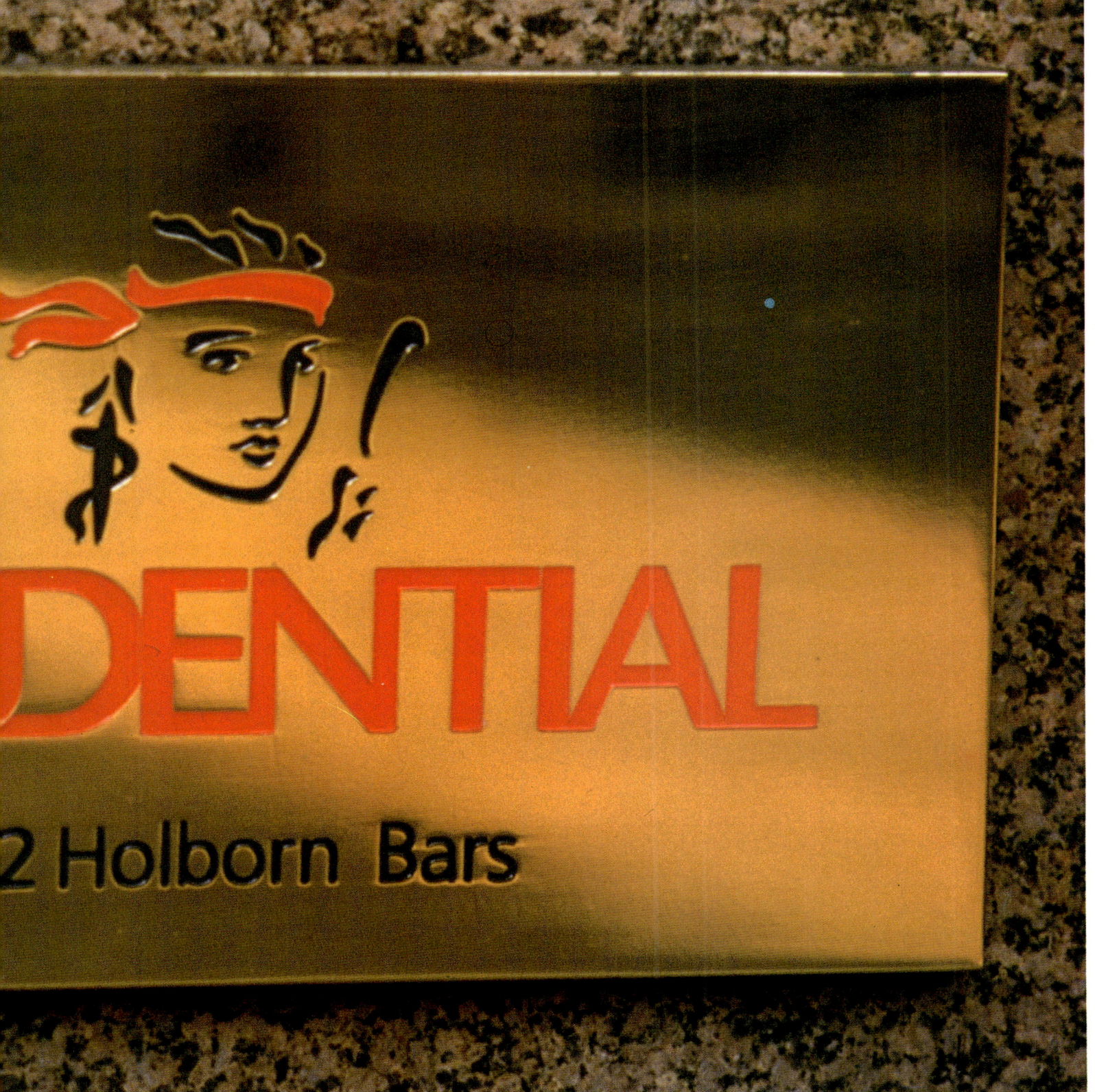

58 PRUDENTIAL CORPORATION

Logotype and mark for general use

Logotype and mark only for specific corporate use

Entrance to city office

City office

Local office

60 PRUDENTIAL CORPORATION

Prudential Property Services "for sale" sign

Prudential Property Services "sold" sign

Prudential Property Services

PRUDENTIAL CORPORATION   61

Items for launch of new corporate
identity: corporate brochure, identity
booklet, and identity video

Product brochures

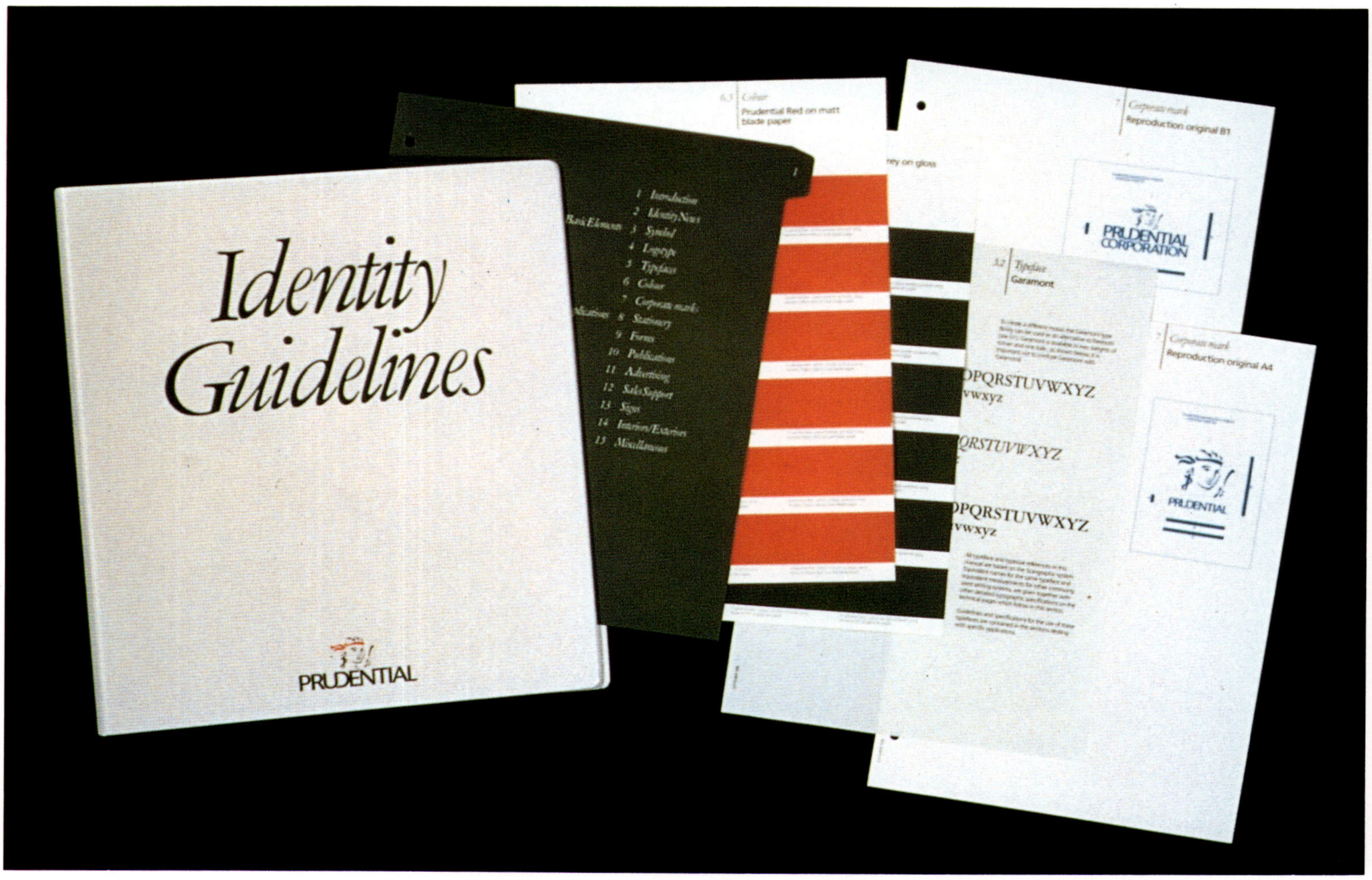

62 PRUDENTIAL CORPORATION

Identity manual

Stationery

PRUDENTIAL CORPORATION   63

Corporate brochure cover and inside spread

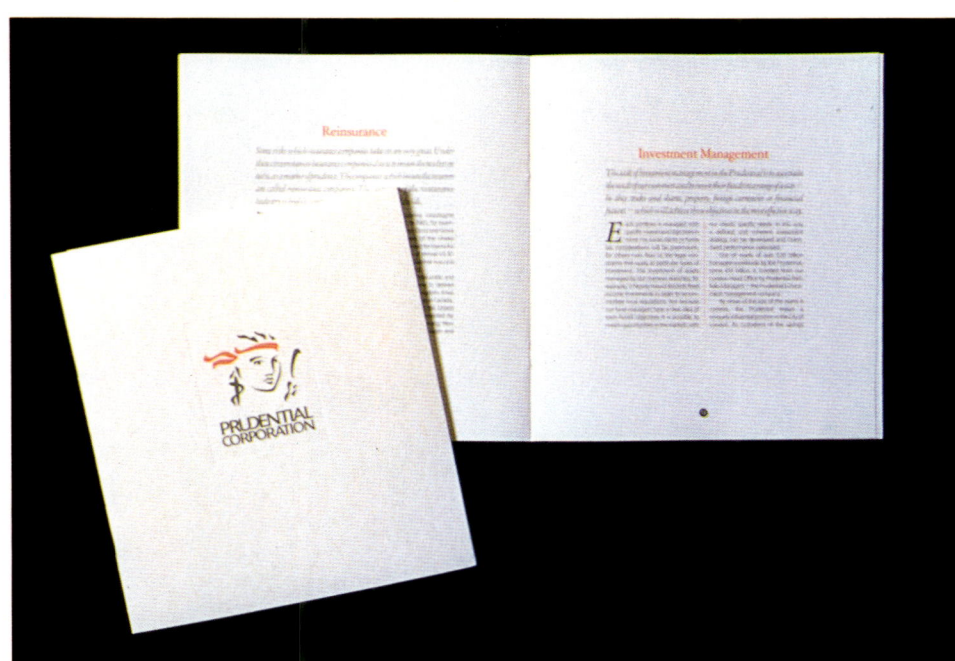

Identity booklet

64   PRUDENTIAL CORPORATION

Silk headscarves

Hard hat

Billboard advertisement

Corporate ties woven of silk and polyester silk

Promotional items — game and matches

UNIVERSITIES

PennState

HEADQUARTERS:	University Park, Pennsylvania
BUSINESS:	Higher education
ORGANIZATION:	65,000 students, 12,000 employees, 22 campuses
DESIGN:	Dixon & Parcels Associates, Inc.
FUNCTIONS OF DESIGN PROGRAM:	Unified identity for institutional visual communications, and licensing of Nittany Lion and logotype on wide spectrum of items sold in the bookstore

The Pennsylvania State University, a major university in the United States that was founded in 1855, has a student body of 65,000, employs 13,000 people, and has 275,000 living alumni. In its "Perspective on the '80s," the University states, "PennState's tomorrow shall be better than today because we are determined that it must be so. We are proud that we want the best and are willing to change to guarantee it."

Driven by this philosophy and the desire to have a single graphic image for all its visual communications, the Intercollegiate Athletic Department of The Pennsylvania State University engaged Dixon & Parcels Associates, Inc., an internationally known marketing and design firm, to help achieve its communications objectives.

In tackling this challenge, Dixon & Parcels surveyed the many identification systems of major United States colleges and universities. This research revealed that more than 125 schools used a member of the cat family to identify their institutions in intercollegiate competition. It became obvious that for the "Nittany Lion" to stand apart from the "cats" used by other universities and colleges, it would have to be unique, yet simultaneously reflect the dignity and heritage of this famous university.

After analyzing these findings, Dixon & Parcels Associates created a stylistic lion in an oval. This projects an easily recognizable image of strength and dignity in one color in any media and in both large and small sizes. Inspiration for this new design came from the famous Nittany Lion statue on the PennState campus sculpted by Heinz Warneke.

Further research focused on the way the student body, the alumni, and the press referred to PennState. Common verbal usage treated Penn State as one word ... "Pennstate." Based on this usage, it was decided that the words "PennState" would be presented as one word with the middle "S" capitalized. This logo is designed in a contemporary style with italic letters to project the forward-looking philosophy of all departments of the university.

One of the stadium press boxes

This focused program of identification not only resulted in clear and singular communication to the various audiences of the University, but it also helped make possible a strong and enforceable licensing program. PennState licenses the use of its "Nittany Lion" and logotype on a wide range of items in the University Book Store from textbook covers to jewelry and sweatshirts. The new ability to enforce a licensing program has developed annual royalties in excess of $200,000 which are distributed for scholarship purposes.

In designing this identification program for the Intercollegiate Athletic Department of PennState, Dixon & Parcels used the same comprehensive research and design approach it uses in all assignments. It is an approach that relies on creativity, as well as pre-design and post-design research, to ensure that the resulting design meets the established objectives.

72 PennState

Inspiration for the "Nittany Lion" trademark

74 PennState

Stationery

Game program

Promotional materials

Magazine cover

76 PennState

Poster

The new logo in China

Logo on megaphone

Football stadium

Jewelry — lapel pin

Aston University

HEADQUARTERS:	Aston, Birmingham, England
BUSINESS:	Higher education
ORGANIZATION:	3,949 students
DESIGN:	Wolff Olins
FUNCTIONS OF DESIGN PROGRAM:	Consistency of institutional identity in graphics, stationery, publications, interiors, and coordination of architecture and landscaping

Aston University, in Birmingham, England, is a technological university with a new science park. Formerly called the University of Aston in Birmingham, Wolff Olins recommended the change of name to Aston University and introduced the concept of the Aston Triangle.

The Triangle is both place (the complex is bounded by three roads) and symbol: blue for the university, red for the science park, and split red and blue for the Aston Triangle. The identity is reinforced in the handling of three key aspects of the site: its entrances (high towers), focus points (pavilions), and boundary (a new signing system). The design program covers stationery, brochures, and architecture.

ASTON UNIVERSITY 81

Triangle plate mounted on metal beam

Logotype

Folders

82 ASTON UNIVERSITY

Tower monument on campus

Detail of mark

New tower monument and existing buildings

Old logotype

ASTON UNIVERSITY   85

New entrance portico and signs

New logo and mark on entrance signs to campus

86 ASTON UNIVERSITY

New elevator tower extension

New entrance portico and signs

Stationery

Stationery — letterheads

Compliments slip and business cards

Stationery — back of envelope

Envelope

Cover of undergraduate bulletin/catalog

Detail of large-scale mark

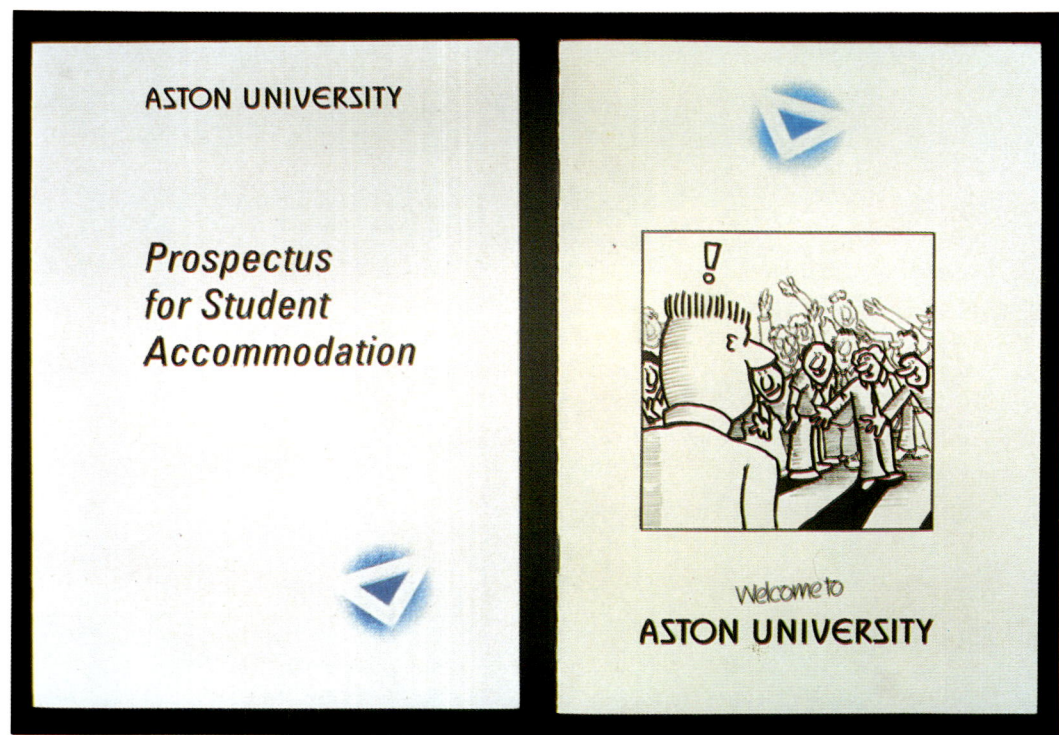

Cover of "Prospectus for Student Accommodation"

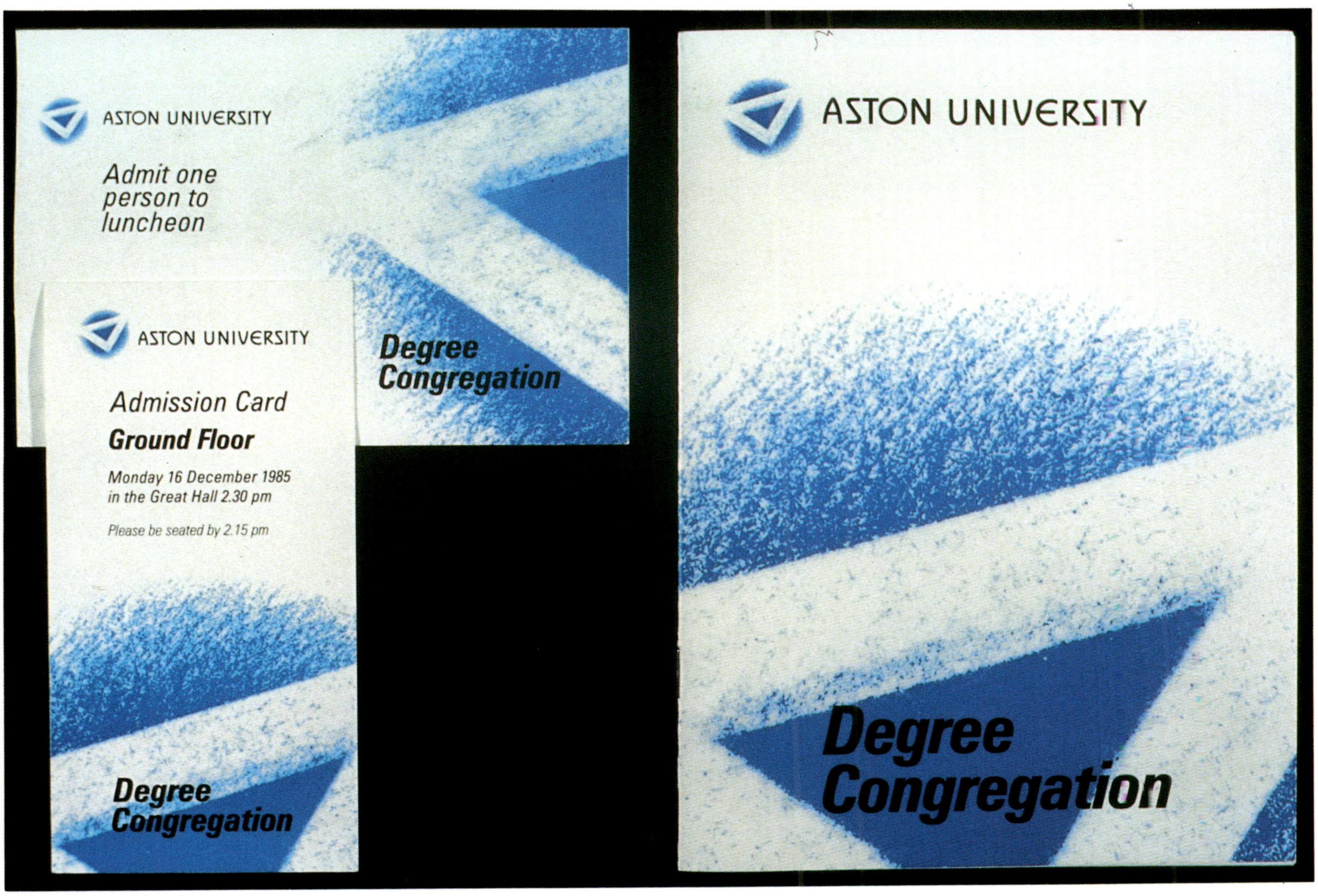

Invitation, admission card, and brochure cover

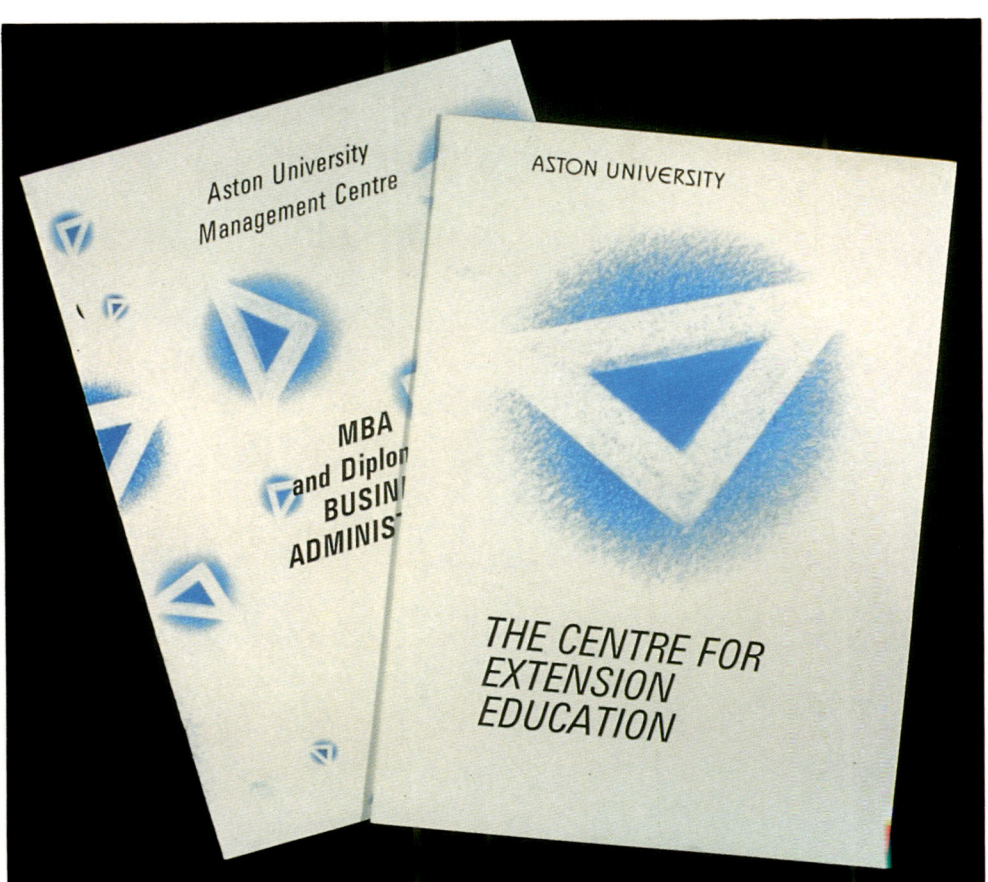

Brochures

GLASS MANUFACTURING

Pilkington

HEADQUARTERS:	St. Helens, Lancashire, England
BUSINESS:	Glass and related product manufacturing
ORGANIZATION:	World's largest glass manufacturing company, subsidiaries in the U.S. and Europe
DESIGN:	Wolff Olins
FUNCTIONS OF DESIGN PROGRAM:	Consistency of corporate identity

Pilkington developed the revolutionary float process for manufacturing flat glass. Today, not only is the company the world's largest manufacturer of float glass, but as a result of diversification, it now also produces a wide range of glass-related products.

This transformation did not happen organically. For the most part, it resulted from acquisitions, and because Pilkington retained all the identities of the companies it took over, the company ultimately faced an identity problem. The true size and nature of the new Pilkington was not apparent. The company was still regarded as simply a flat glass manufacturer. Few were aware of the high-technology and added-value products that it now produced.

The new identity now being adopted will not only present the group of companies and the individual companies in an appropriate way but will also reveal the diversity and strength of Pilkington to all of the company's audiences.

Sign

Corporate mark

Corporate flag

Logotype and corporate mark

Old logotype and mark

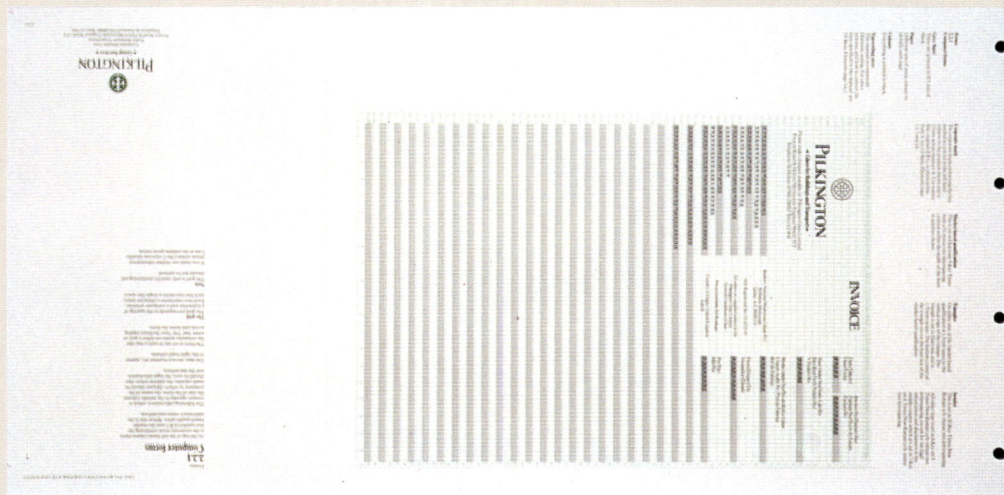

Pages from corporate design manual

Typeface — "Pilkington Times" — for headline use

ABCDEFGHIJKLM
NOPQRSTUVWXYZ
ABCDEFGHIJKLM
NOPQRSTUVWXYZ
ÅÃÂÀÁÆÄÐÇÊÈÉËĞÍÏÎÌ
ŁÑŒÔÓÖÓÕØŞÙÚÛÜ
abcdefghijklmnopqrstuvwxyz
àâåãáäæçđêéèë fi ffi fl ffl ff
ğíîìïıłñôõóòøöœşùúûüß
£1234567890$¢%*.,:;""!?-()/&§«»

Pages from corporate design manual

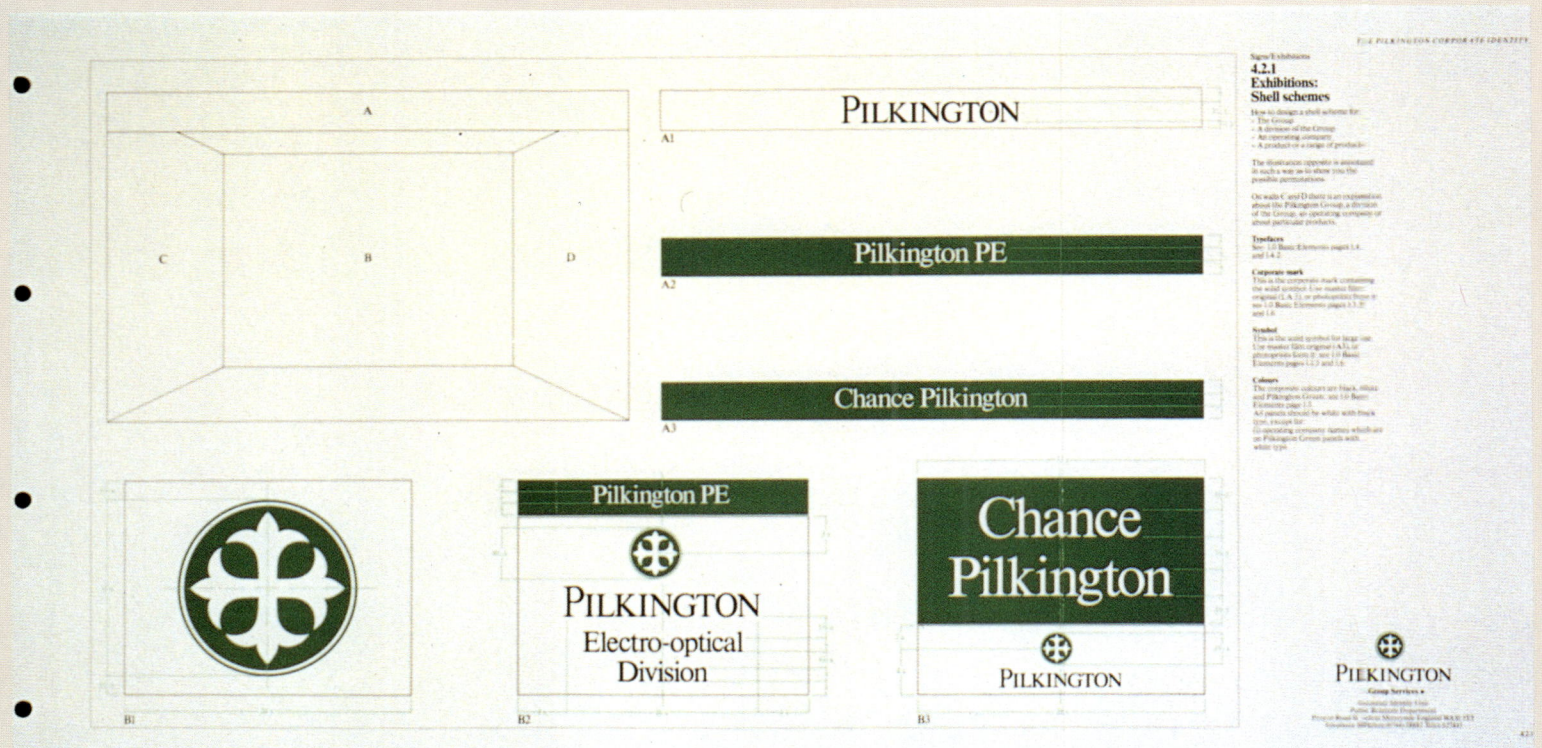

Stationery

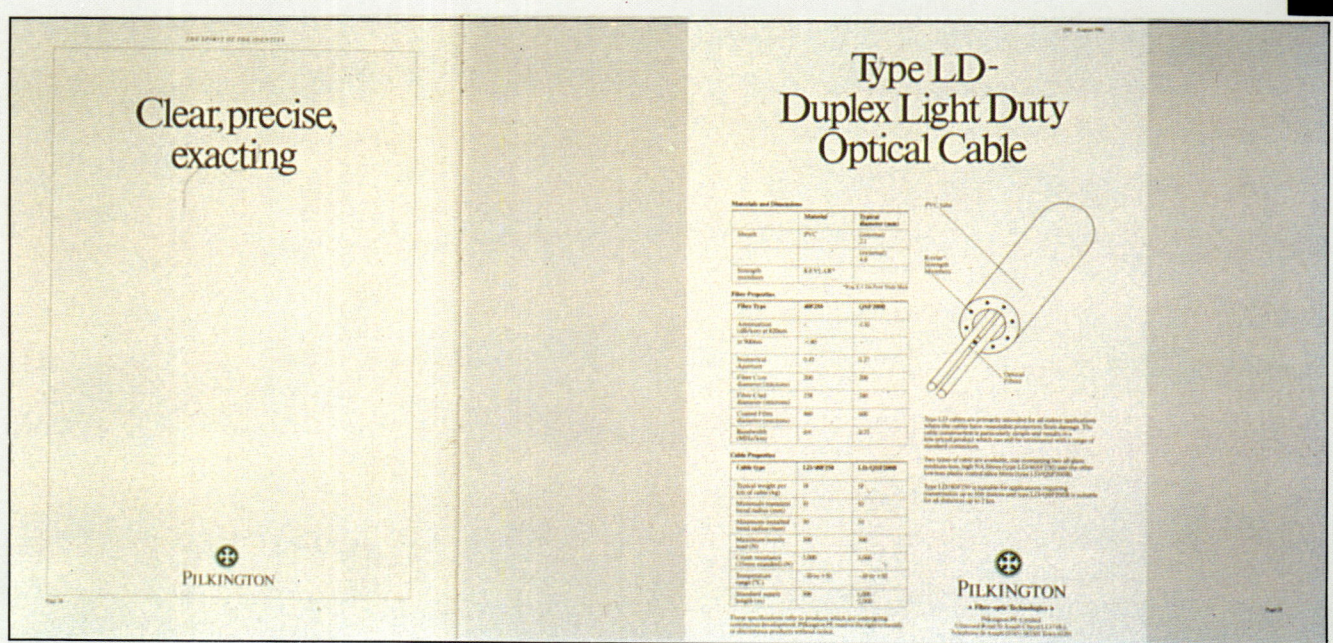

Product diagram and chart

Folder and product leaflets

Corporate identity manual

Advertisement

Advertisement

Product advertisement

Product advertisement

106 PILKINGTON

"An even better way to say insulation" print media product ad

Series of print media ads beginning with "British Company Wins French Lottery"

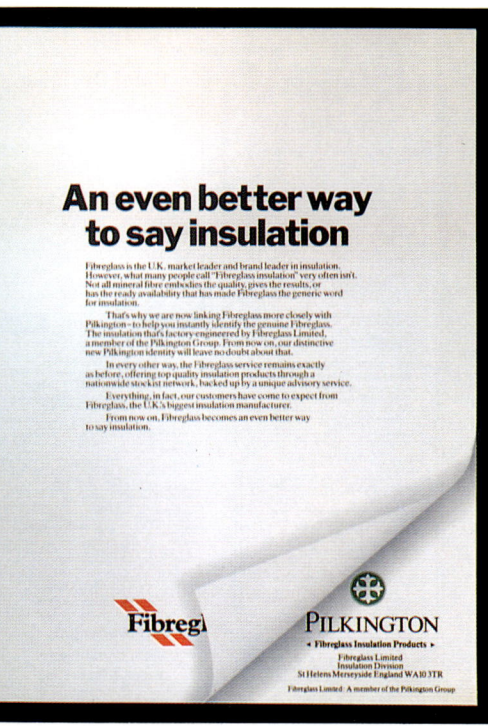

"Graduate Opportunities in 1987" recruitment brochure

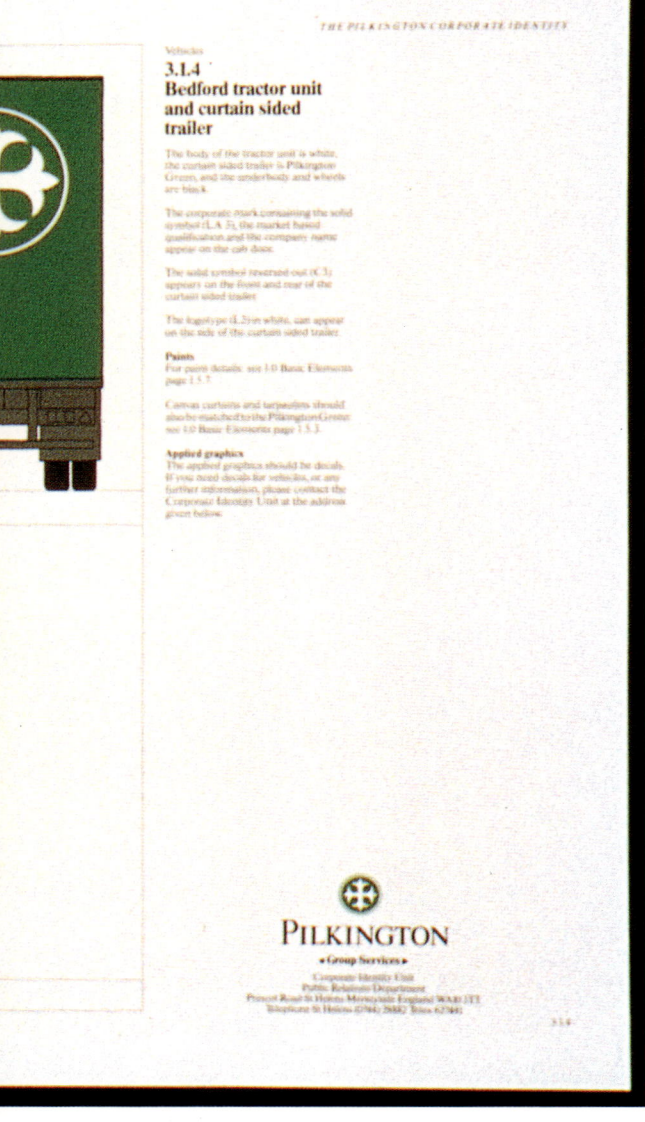

Company vehicle logo specification page from design manual

Freestanding outdoor directional signage

Wall-mounted exterior directional signage

Wall-mounted identifying signage

Exterior directional freestanding signage

Reception area showing corporate mark on glass panel

Corporate mark on rear doors of vehicle

Logotype and corporate mark on company vehicle

Logotype and corporate mark on company vehicle

Corporate mark on rear of vehicle

Logotype on company vehicle

Product advertisement

Spread from recruitment brochure

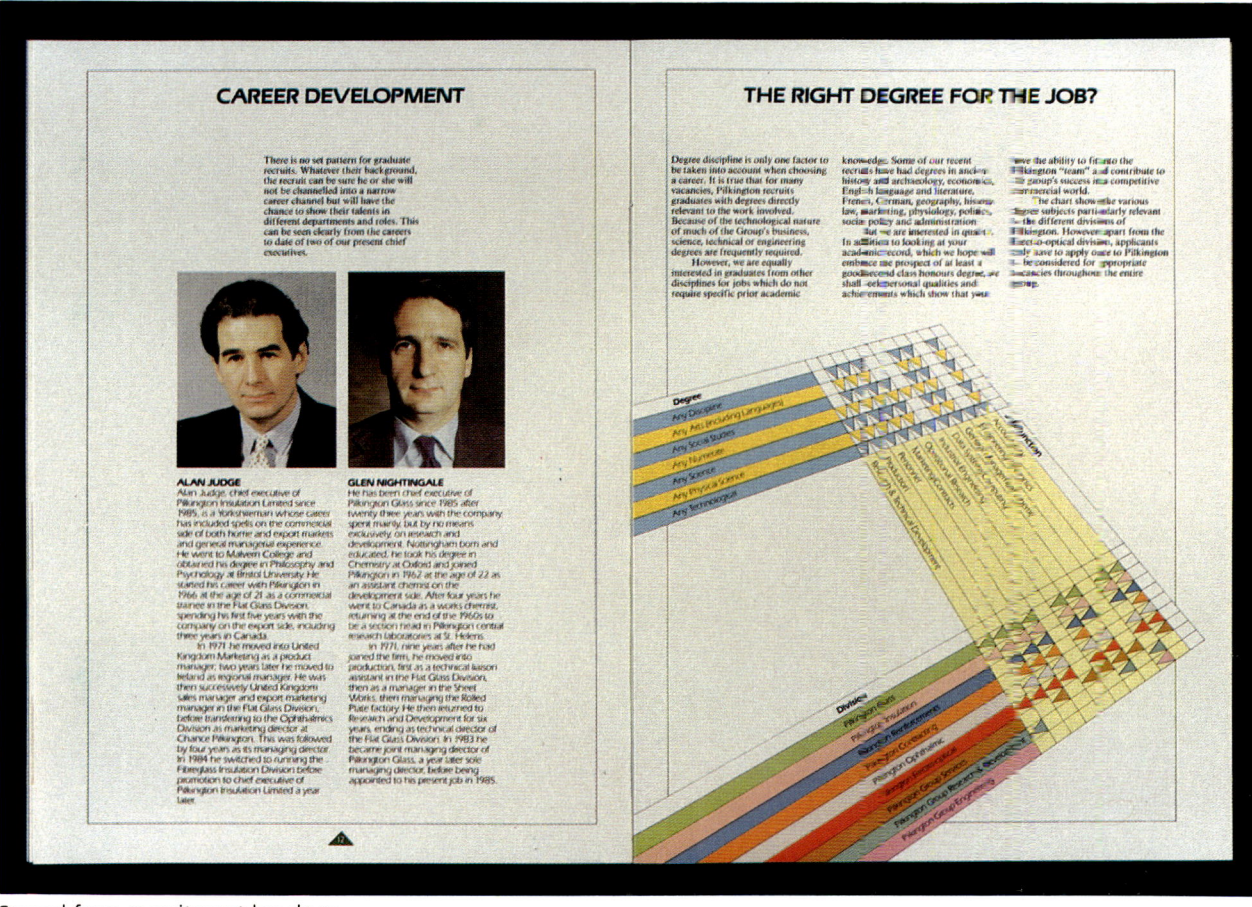

Spread from recruitment brochure

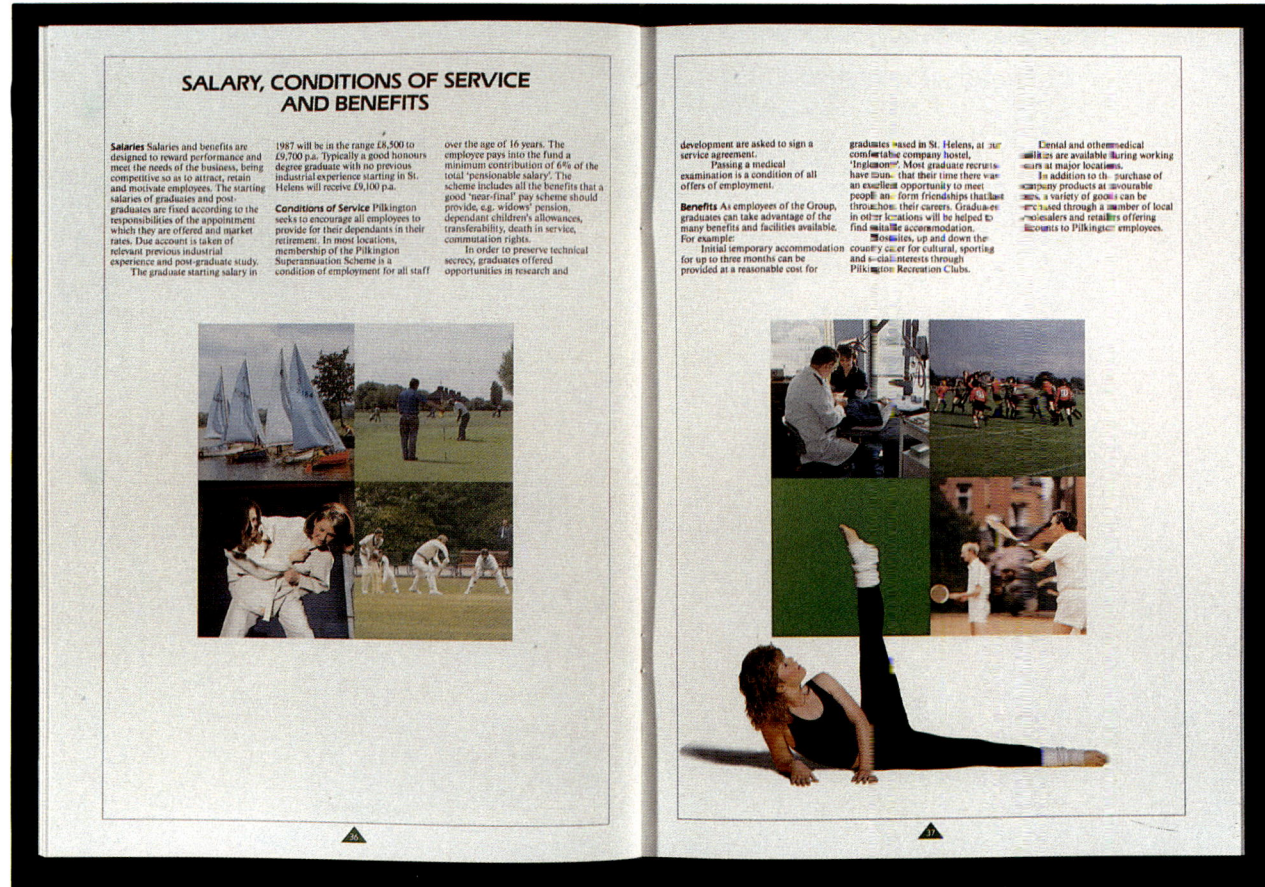

Spread from annual report

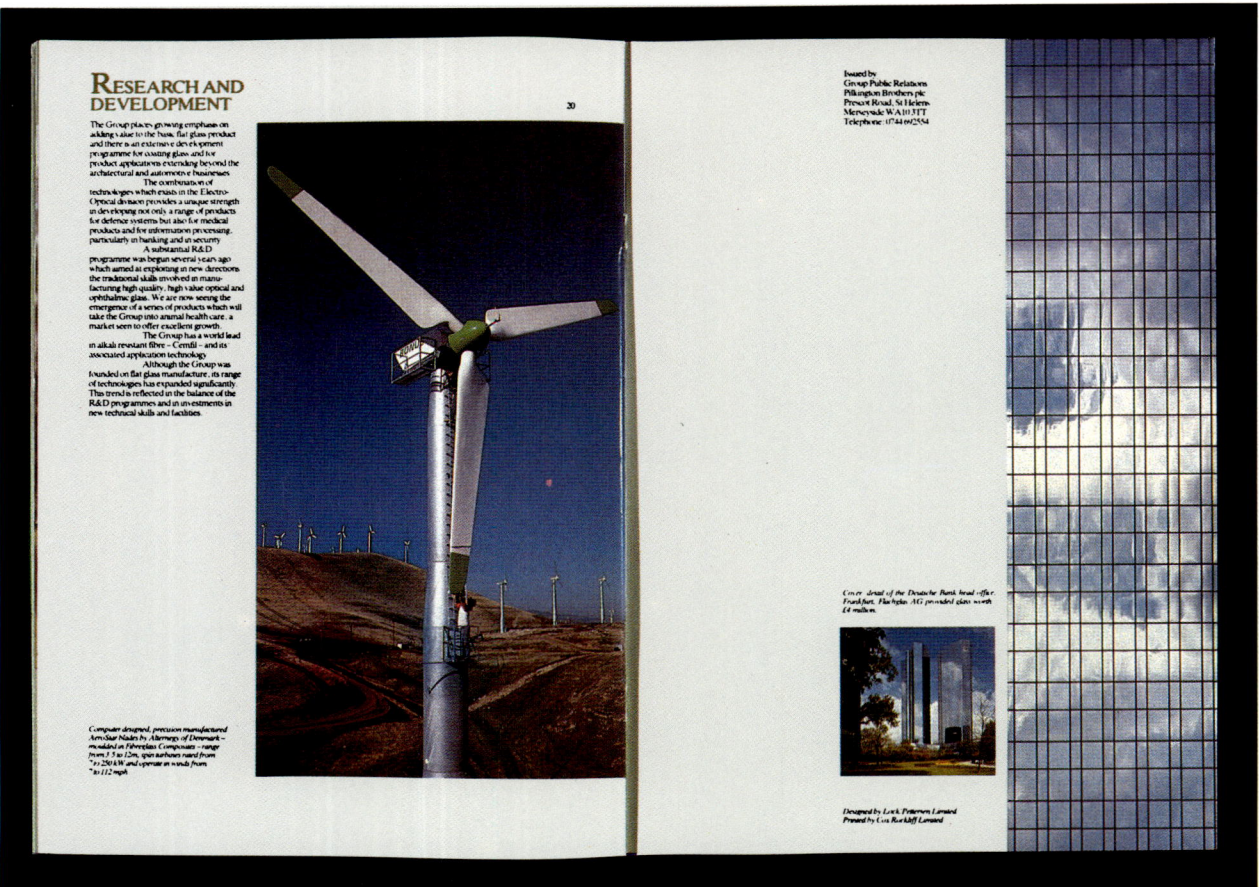

Spread from annual report

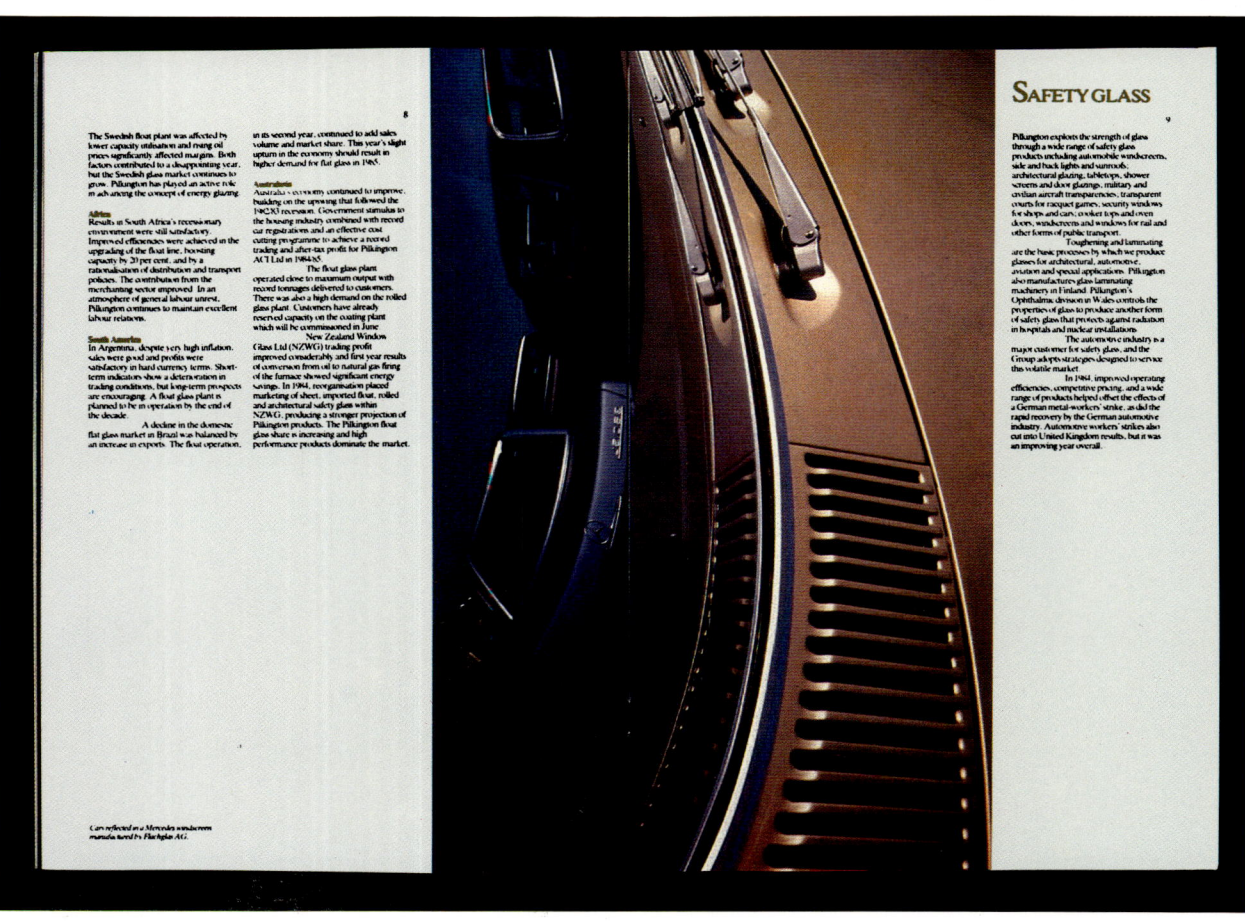

Annual report cover

PRINTING

Gavin Martin

HEADQUARTERS: London, England
BUSINESS: Printing
ORGANIZATION: One branch, 30 employees
DESIGN: Wolff Olins
FUNCTIONS OF DESIGN PROGRAM: Consistency of corporate identity

Gavin Martin, formed in the late 1960s, had become a well-established color printer for the art and design industries. In 1986 Wolff Olins was asked to look at the company's identity. The result was to create an image of a company that recognizes and appreciates design and is aware of the designer's needs from both technical and visual points of view.

Logotype on light and dark backgrounds

Folder and newsletter cover

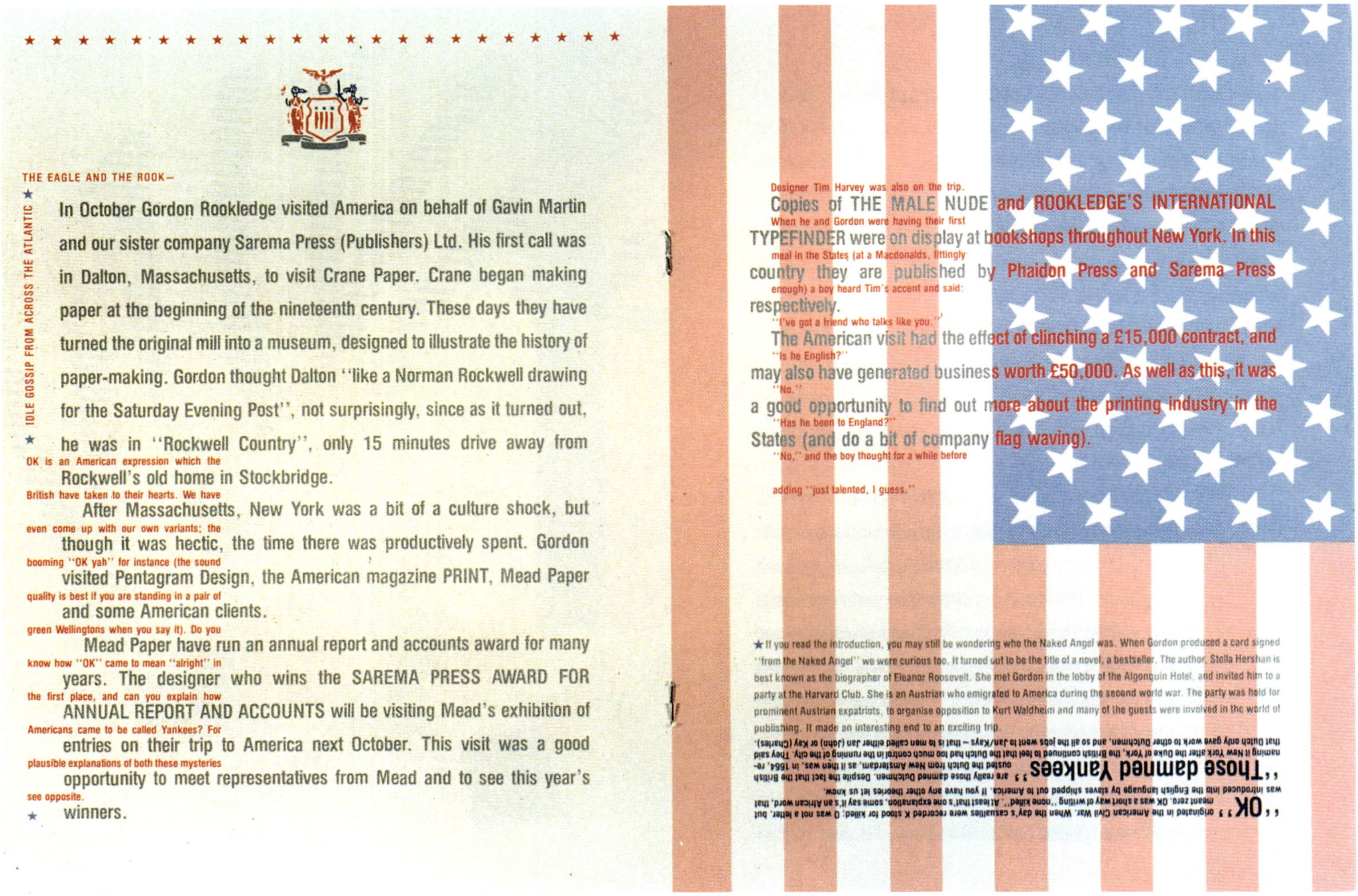

124 GAVIN MARTIN

Inside spread of newsletter

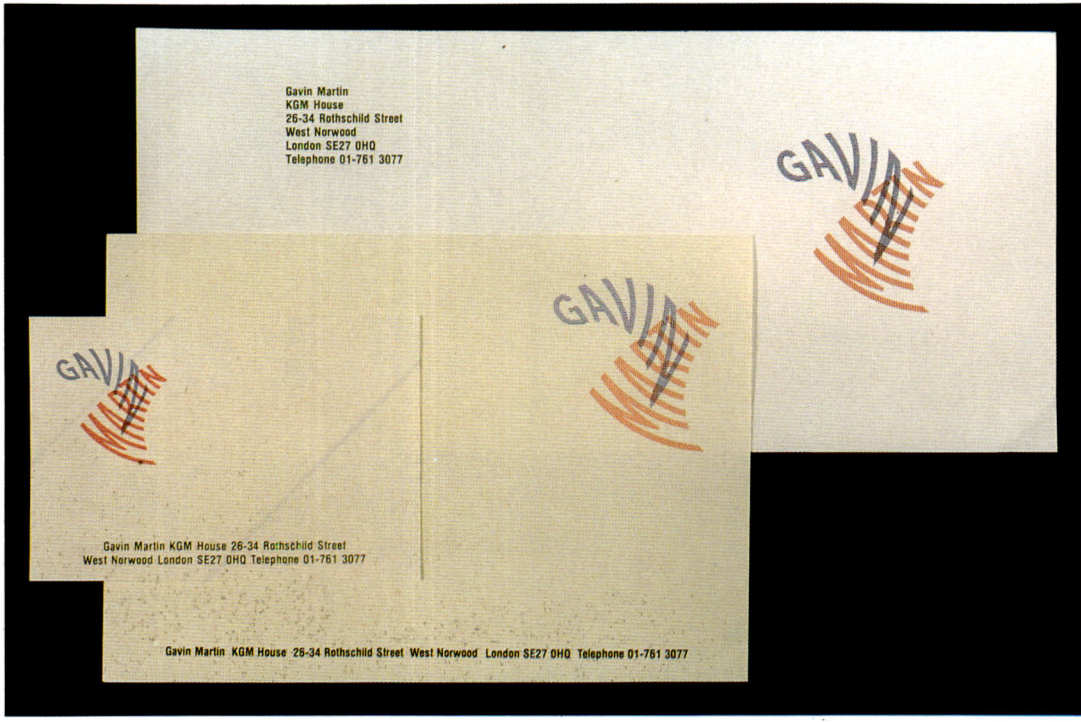

Compliments slip and adhesive labels

GAVIN MARTIN 125

OUR NEW IDENTITY

Our new logo, Gavin Martin in red and blue, has been designed for us by Stuart Jane of Wolff Olins. Like David Tuhill, he studied at the Royal College of Art. When Gordon Rookledge taught print production at the College, Stuart was one of his students, and he has worked for Gavin Martin in the past. He designed News Bulletin 10 (known to connoisseurs as "the long narrow one with the tortoise"). After graduating from the RCA in 1983 he joined Wolff Olins. For his first year he worked there full-time, now he combines four days a week for them with freelance projects (this bulletin, for instance).

Did you go to the Graphics Exhibition in October? It was held at the Business Design Centre, London's newest exhibition venue and a building that's well worth a visit in its own right. If you did go, you might have got a sneak preview of Gavin Martin's new stationery, on the stand of ISTD Fine Paper. The certificate for The Sarema Press Annual Report and Accounts was also on display. Thank you everyone who 'phoned up to say how much you liked them. Though we visited the exhibition we hadn't spotted them ourselves and didn't know they were there until the calls started coming in!

As we mentioned in the last edition of the bulletin the logo is only one part of a whole new look for Gavin Martin. The changes taking place here are more than cosmetic, they reflect a company with plans for expansion. There will be more information in subsequent bulletins, or you could ask anyone wearing one of our new GM ties!.

Spread from newsletter announcing new identity

Business cards

Gavin Martin

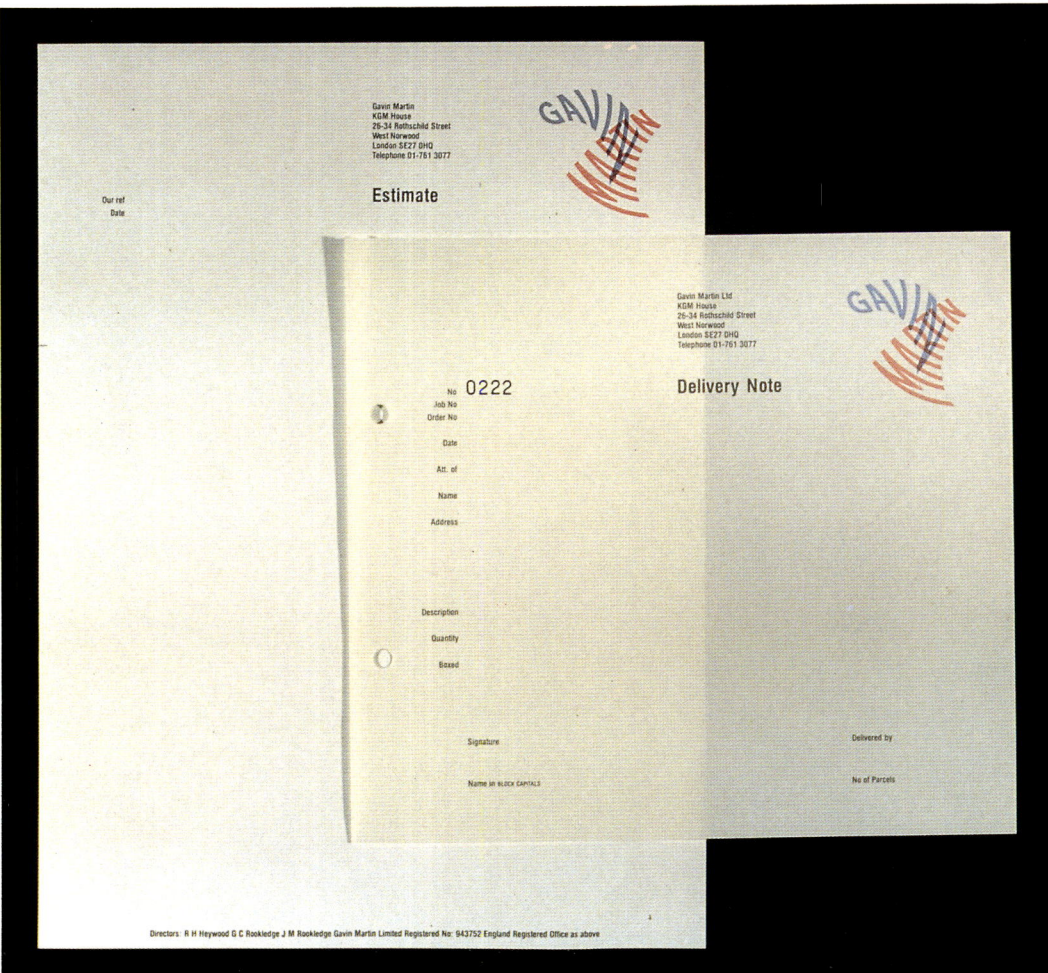

Estimate and delivery forms

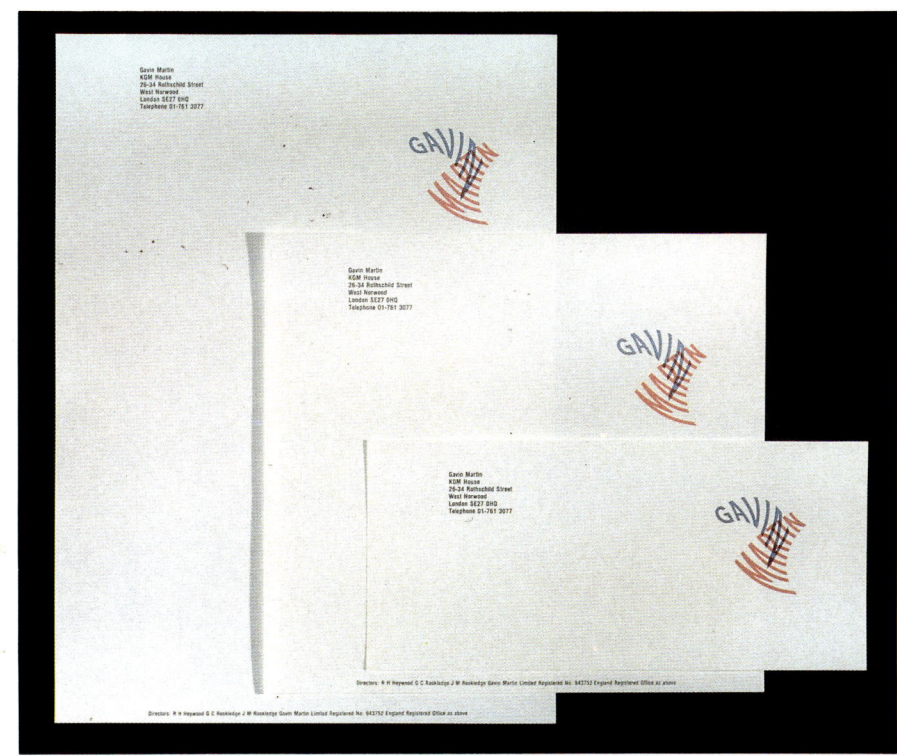

Range of stationery

Inside spread of newsletter

Folder and stationery

HEALTH CARE

Mount Carmel Health

HEADQUARTERS:	Columbus, Ohio
BUSINESS:	Health care
ORGANIZATION:	550 physicians, 3,000 employees, hospital affiliates throughout Central Ohio
DESIGN:	Salvato & Coe
FUNCTIONS OF DESIGN PROGRAM:	Unified identity for corporate visual communications, and distinctive market image for the hospital and its subsidiaries

After the Civil War, the Sisters of the Holy Cross began to open hospitals in various parts of the country. On July 16, 1886, in Columbus, Ohio, one of those hospitals was dedicated to Our Lady of Mount Carmel and was named Hawkes Hospital of Mount Carmel, in honor of its founder, Dr. Hawkes.

Today, Mount Carmel Health is a growing network of health care facilities, with a medical staff of 550 physicians, more than 3,000 employees, and hospital affiliations throughout the Central Ohio region.

Early in 1984, a corporate restructuring cleared the way for the rapid business diversification and aggressive marketing thrusts needed for Mount Carmel Health to become a competitive regional health care provider.

Later that year, Sister Gladys Marie, CSC, President of the organization, created a marketing department and initiated a corporate design program. The primary goal was to create a unified identity and a distinctive market image for Mount Carmel Health and its subsidiaries. A secondary goal was to create a unique family look for all corporate visual communications.

The Columbus-based design firm of Salvato and Coe worked closely with senior management and members of the marketing team to design, develop, and implement the Mount Carmel Health corporate program. After corporate restructuring, the new holding company was named Mount Carmel Health to capitalize on the market equity of the Mount Carmel name and to emphasize the "holistic health" focus of the organization.

A corporate symbol that embodied the radiant spiritual quality of the Sisters of the Holy Cross was designed to graphically unify all corporate subsidiaries. A standard system of typefaces was utilized to create a family look for all logotypes, descriptive nomenclature, and copy. The corporate colors of burgundy and beige were used to enhance the unified look in graphic applications ranging from transportation fleets to campus scale architectural upgrades.

A visual communications program was designed and implemented for a full spectrum of products and services. Compelling graphic formats, together with warm photographic treatments and copy styles, were used to create the "warm and caring" image and market position for Mount Carmel Health. This market positioning was advanced by "The Spirit of Life" and "The Spirit at Work" campaigns, which emphasized to the public and employees respectively those important humanistic qualities of Mount Carmel Health.

Corporate diversification and expansion continues with a growing roster of new products and services for the next century at Mount Carmel Health. It will be the century of "High Tech" and "High Touch" in the health care industry, and these industry themes will serve as the foundation of the next generation of projects in the Mount Carmel corporate design program.

MT. CARMEL HEALTH   133

Illuminated glass atrium with stylized corporate symbol atop the Mount Carmel Medical Center and corporate offices

Site identification signage for a typical primary care facility

DESIGN CREDITS

Graphics:	Salvato & Coe Associates Inc.
Photography:	Roman Sapecki
Copystyle:	Al Romano, Consultant
Exhibits:	Boss Displays; Charles O'Connor, Consultant
Architecture & Interiors:	Karlsburger + Associates Architects Inc.
Glass Atrium & Exteriors:	Bohm NBBJ
Wall Sculpture:	Bill Malis, Artist; Nancy Johnson, Art Consultant
Computer Animation:	Cranston/Csuri; Neil Pynchon, Consultant

134 MOUNT CARMEL HEALTH

Commissioned wall sculpture of corporate symbol in the new Medical Staff Building lobby

Site identification signage at the Mount Carmel Medical Center entrance

The new Mount Carmel Health 500-seat auditorium with stained glass windows salvaged from the original chapel

Corporate colors of burgundy and beige applied to building exteriors of the Mount Carmel Medical Center

Four story atrium area above the Medical Staff Building lobby

Physicians' lounge in the Medical Staff Building

Glass wall in physicians' lounge looking into atrium area of Medical Staff Building

140   MOUNT CARMEL HEALTH

Graphic identity on Biomedical Services van

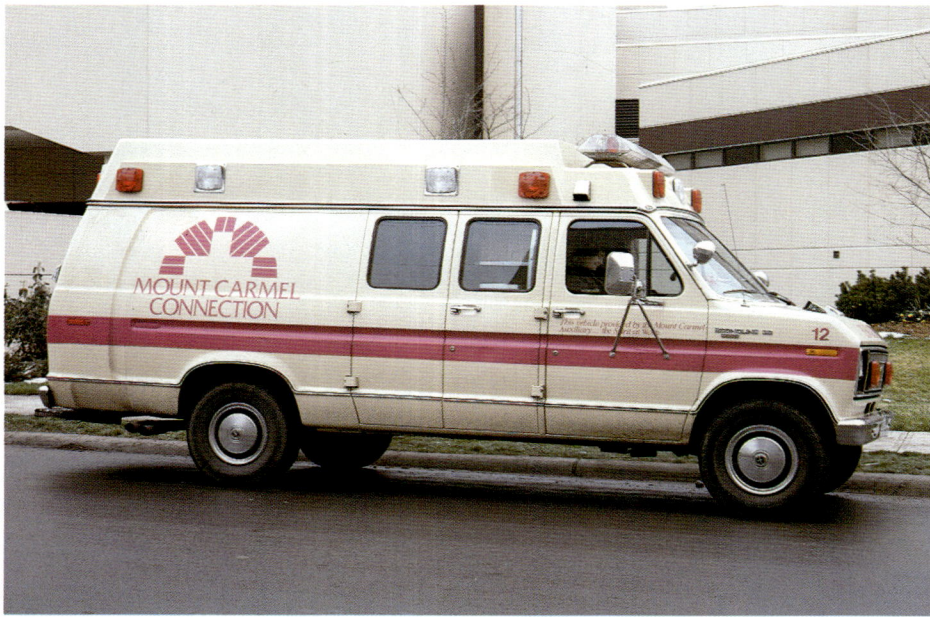

The Mount Carmel Connection ambulance graphics

Mount Carmel Health security services vehicle

The Ohio Heart and Vascular Mobile Diagnostic Lab with Institute symbol and logotype

Entrance to Health Horizons retail store

Interior of Health Horizons retail store featuring durable medical equipment and services

142 MOUNT CARMEL HEALTH

Imagine campaign print advertisement using computer generated graphic image from television advertisement

Our computers make fast friends.

In trauma cases, saving seconds in obtaining vital information is often tantamount to saving lives. That's why at Mount Carmel Health, some of your fastest friends are computers.

On arrival, trauma victims are immediately linked to our computer-based monitoring and telecommunications system, in place at only a few other hospitals in the country.

The system not only provides Emergency personnel with continuous readouts of all vital signs but *simultaneously* transmits this information to other critical care areas in the hospital.

Armed with a total picture of the patient's condition, how the problem is progressing, and the effects of medication administered, these specialists are prepared for swift, appropriate action the second the patient arrives.

The point is simple. In trauma cases, our computers are more than friendly. They're your fast friends for life.

MOUNT CARMEL HEALTH
CENTENNIAL CELEBRATION
1886–1986

A MEMBER OF THE HOLY CROSS HEALTH SYSTEM

Corporate trade show panel showing Imagine campaign graphic

MOUNT CARMEL HEALTH 143

The Ohio Heart and Vascular Institute trade show exhibit showing Imagine campaign heart graphics

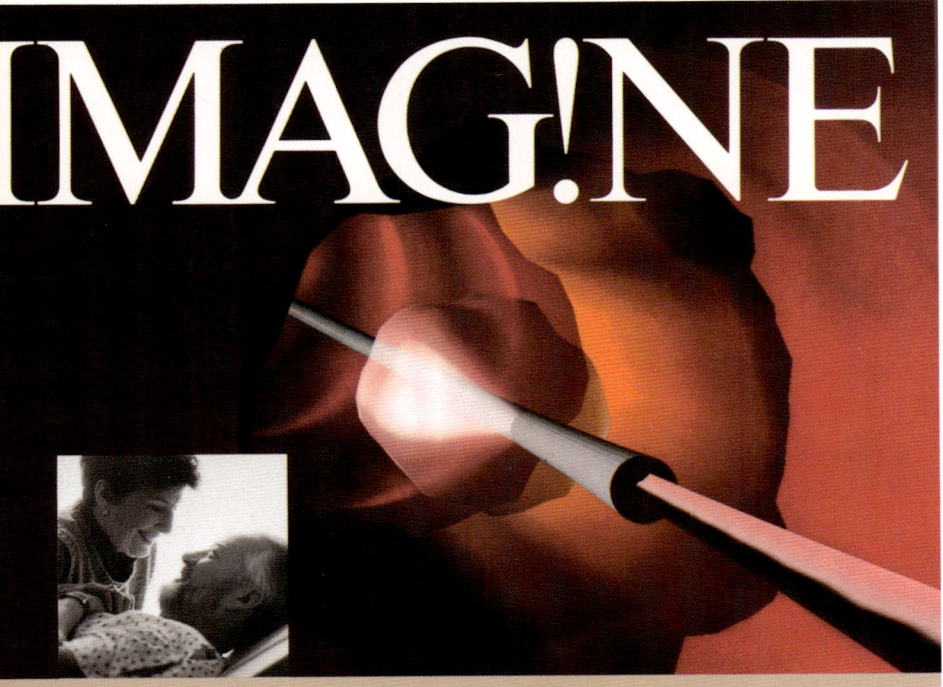

IMAG!NE

We let your heart be the guide.

Coronary disease? Open heart surgery is one approach. But there's an alternative: PTCA, pioneered in the midwest by Mount Carmel's Medical Staff.

Which procedure to use when? Simple. With medical staff expertise in both, we let your patient's heart be the guide.

Cardiology isn't the only area where Mount Carmel Health physicians are setting the pace. They're at the forefront in orthopedics, gerontology and oncology. In trauma care. And in the treatment of Alzheimer's disease and diabetes.

This year we're celebrating a century in health care. One of our greatest sources of pride as we look back is that our medical staff has always looked so far ahead.

MOUNT CARMEL HEALTH
CENTENNIAL CELEBRATION
1886-1986

A MEMBER OF THE HOLY CROSS HEALTH SYSTEM

A computer generated graphic used both in print and on television to promote Mount Carmel's leadership in heart and vascular services

144   MOUNT CARMEL HEALTH

Regional trade show exhibition used to market Mount Carmel Health services to other hospitals

The Imagine print advertisement featuring the pioneering Alzheimer's Center at Mount Carmel Health

We're putting the best minds to work on Alzheimer's.

Outstanding care for Alzheimer's patients is now closer at hand, thanks to the opening of the Alzheimer's Center at Mount Carmel.

This uniquely comprehensive resource would not be a reality without the vision and pioneering spirit of our medical staff.

This year we're celebrating a century in health care. Looking back, we can see many areas where Mount Carmel Health physicians have set the pace. In cardiology, orthopedics, gerontology and oncology. In trauma care. And in the treatment of diabetes.

Now, with the Alzheimer's Center, our medical staff will be at the forefront in exploring facets of the mind that have long surpassed the mind's understanding.

MOUNT CARMEL HEALTH
CENTENNIAL CELEBRATION
1886-1986

A MEMBER OF THE HOLY CROSS HEALTH SYSTEM

MOUNT CARMEL HEALTH   145

A three-dimensional networking model showing the linking capability of the Mount Carmel Health Remote Cardiac Monitoring service concept

Entrance to the 60-foot by 20-foot corporate trade show exhibit which illustrates the partnership approach to affiliations

"Brand Identity" developed for the Ohio Heart and Vascular Institute printed materials

146 MOUNT CARMEL HEALTH

Cover of *Come to Life,* to large-format publication featuring a "Centennial History in The Spirit of Mount Carmel"

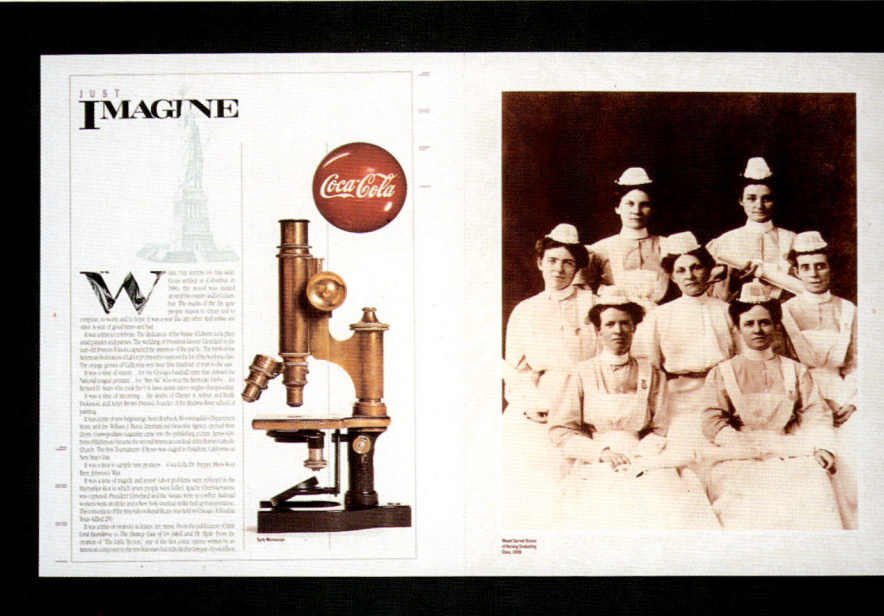

Example of unique design treatment of historic information in *Come to Life*

Feature story treatment used in the quarterly *Spirit of Life* corporate magazine

Spirit of Life profile story about Dr. Cooney, past President of the Mount Carmel Health Medical Staff

Examples of Physician Referral print advertisements featuring selected members of the Mount Carmel Health Medical Staff

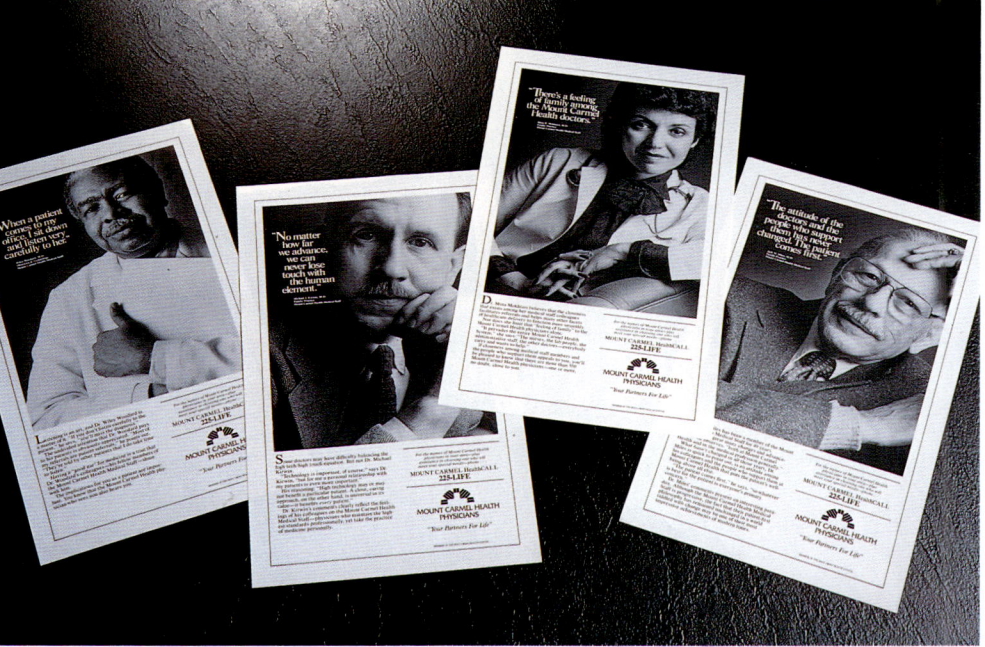

Spirit of Life profile story about Michael Anthony, M.D., illustrating the humanistic aspects of practicing medicine

148 MOUNT CARMEL HEALTH

Poster used to promote a tribute to the Mount Carmel Health Medical Staff

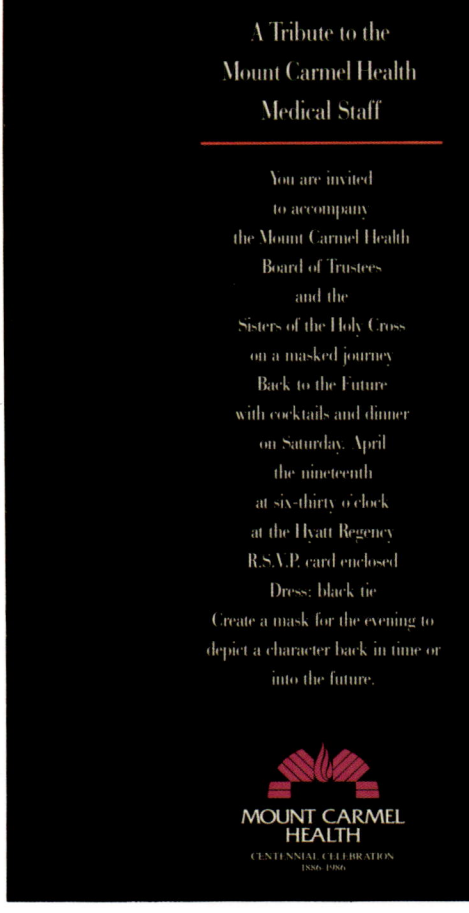

Poster used to promote the *Come to Life* Centennial theme among employees

The Spirit of Life corporate publication, which has won many national and international awards

Guest invitation to a tribute to the Mount Carmel Health Medical Staff

MOUNT CARMEL HEALTH 149

Ideas poster used to promote the Bright Ideas campaign among employees in preparation for the Centennial celebration

150 MOUNT CARMEL HEALTH

A Blast From the Past poster used to promote the employee Centennial party

Touch the Future promotional poster used to invite Ohio Hospital Association members to the Mount Carmel Health exhibition, which launched the corporate Affiliation Program

Theme area of corporate exhibition featuring widely acclaimed mime artist, Gregg Goldston, as "Your Silent Partner"

MOUNT CARMEL HEALTH   151

Medical Staff Outreach and Development Services area of the corporate trade show exhibit

Large photographic exhibit mural of Mount Carmel Health family used to promote the Center for Human Empowerment

"Pathways to Partnerships" promotional poster used to invite Ohio Hospital Association members and Mount Carmel Health affiliates to the corporate exhibition and hospitality program

Unified design developed for product sales literature and point-of-purchase display systems

Corporate exhibition used to introduce the innovative and pathfinding Advanced Treatment and Bionics Institute and The Center for Human Empowerment programs to regional and national healthcare markets

The Bionic Person used in corporate exhibition to illustrate advanced treatment technologies

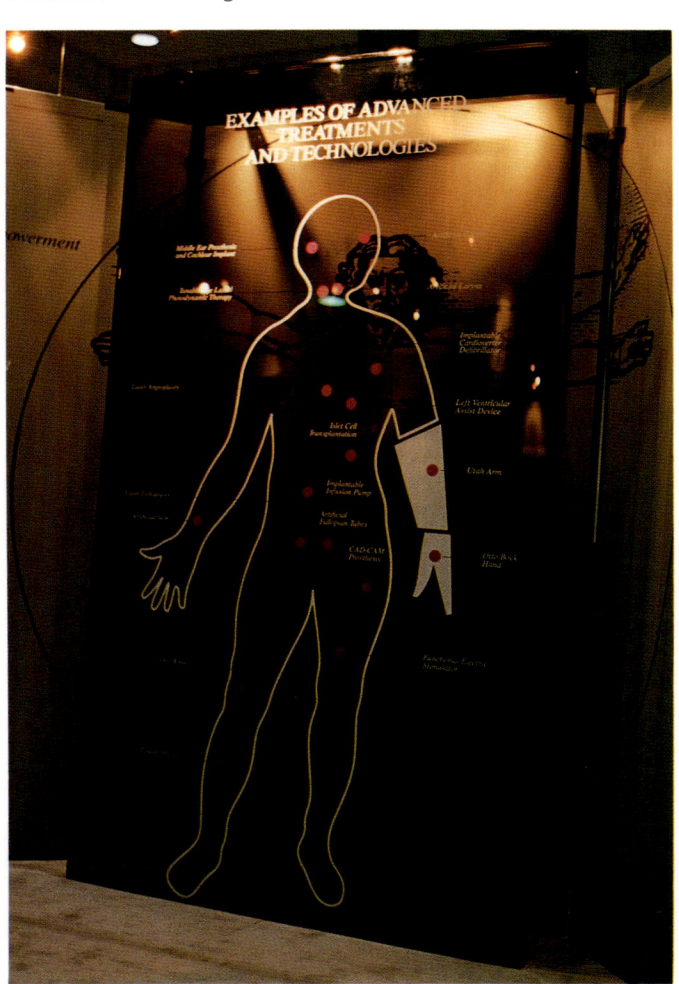

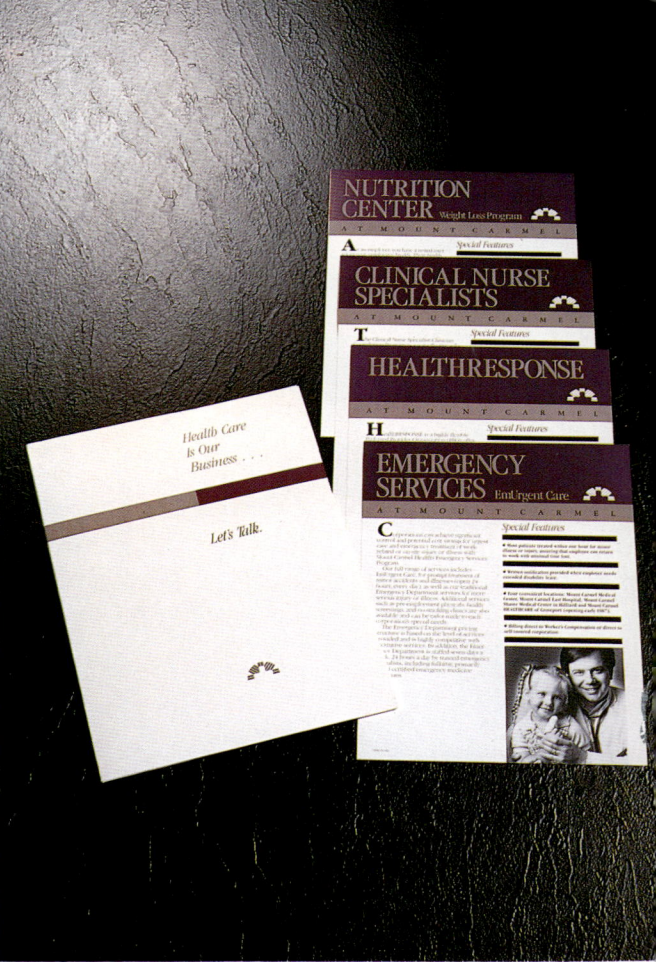

Product specification sheets designed for presentations by corporate sales representatives

"Pathways to Partnerships" theme area of the corporate trade show exhibit

MOUNT CARMEL HEALTH 153

Biomedical services area of the corporate trade show exhibit

Mount Carmel SHARE print materials for alcoholism and chemical dependency programs

"Imagine" coffee mugs with Centennial logo used as promotional items at Centennial celebration events

APPENDIX

This is a standard checklist of items on which logos and other corporate design elements are usually applied. The list is appropriate for most companies, but may need modifying in particular cases.

Products and Services
PRODUCTS
    Product design
    Product identification
    Plates with model and identification numbers
    Operating instructions
    Calibration instructions

PACKAGING
    Inner packaging
    Outer cartons
    Labelling
    Delivery instructions
    Installation instructions

Environments
INTERIORS/EXTERIORS
    Buildings
    Reception areas
    Sales areas
    Offices
    Factories
    Shops
    Showrooms

SIGNS
    Main identification
    General sign system, both internal and external

EXHIBITIONS

CLOTHING
    Badges
    Safety hats
    Overalls
    Lab coats
    Smocks
    Uniforms

Communication Material
STATIONERY
    Letterheads
    Memos
    Complement slips
    Business cards
    Envelopes
    Address labels

FORMS
    Accounting
    Purchasing
    Sales
    Production
    Personnel

PUBLICATIONS
    Corporate
    Personnel and training
    Industry packages
    Product

VEHICLES
    Road vehicles
    Factory vehicles

ADVERTISING
    Corporate
    Recruitment
    Product/service

PROMOTIONS AND GIVEAWAYS
    Flags
    Stickers
    Ties
    Promotional and point of sale material

Excerpted from the Wolff Olins "Guide to Corporate Identity."
Reprinted with permission of Wolff Olins in London, England.

Index I
Applications

ADVERTISING
  Mount Carmel, 142–4, 147
  Pilkington, 104–7, 112
  Prudential Corporation, 65
  Quaker State Corporation, 27, 33

BUILDING, OFFICE, AND FACILITIES GRAPHICS
  Aston University, 81, 83–7
  Mount Carmel Health, 132, 134–9, 141
  PennState, 71
  Pilkington, 109
  Prudential Corporation, 57–9, 60
  Q8 — Kuwait Petroleum International, 39, 40, 42, 46–9

CORPORATE AND ORGANIZATIONAL BROCHURES
  Aston University, 90–1
  Mount Carmel Health, 145, 149, 153
  PennState, 75
  Pilkington, 107, 113–5
  Prudential Corporation, 61, 63

CUSTOMIZED ALPHABETS
  Pilkington, 101
  Quaker State Corporation, 31

IDENTITY/DESIGN MANUALS
  Pilkington, 100–1, 103, 106–7
  Prudential Corporation, 62
  Q8 — Kuwait Petroleum International, 42–3
  Quaker State Corporation, 21-3

LOGOTYPES
  Aston University, 81–2, 84, 90
  Gavin Martin, 121
  PennState, 73
  Pilkington, 101
  Prudential Corporation, 58
  Q8 — Kuwait Petroleum International, 37
  Quaker State Corporation, 21

PRODUCT PACKAGING
  Q8 — Kuwait Petroleum International, 46
  Quaker State Corporation, 24, 26-7, 29, 30, 32

PRODUCT SALES LITERATURE
  Mount Carmel Health, 151–2
  Pilkington, 102–3
  Quaker State Corporation, 25-6, 28, 31

PROMOTIONAL MATERIALS/SALES AIDS
  Mount Carmel Health, 142–5, 148–9, 150–3
  PennState, 76–7
  Prudential Corporation, 64–5
  Q8 — Kuwait Petroleum International, 47
  Quaker State Corporation, 25, 28, 32-3

PUBLICATIONS
  Gavin Martin, 122–5, 127
  Mount Carmel Health, 146–8
  PennState, 74–5
  Q8 — Kuwait Petroleum International, 45

SALES AIDS. See Promotional Materials/Sales Aids.

SIGNAGE
  Aston University, 85
  Mount Carmel Health, 134
  Pilkington, 97–9
  Prudential Corporation, 55, 60
  Q8 — Kuwait Petroleum International, 41

STATIONERY, BUSINESS CARDS, FOLDERS, AND FORMS
  Aston University, 81, 88–9
  Gavin Martin, 124–7
  PennState, 74
  Pilkington, 102, 108–9
  Prudential Corporation, 62
  Q8 — Kuwait Petroleum International, 44–5

VEHICLES
  Mount Carmel Health, 140–1
  Pilkington, 110–1
  Q8 — Kuwait Petroleum International, 48

Index II
Projects

ASTON UNIVERSITY
  Building, offices, and facilities graphics, 81, 83–7
  Logotypes, 81–2, 84, 90
  Organizational brochures, 90–1
  Signage, 85
  Stationery, business cards, folders, and forms, 81, 88–9

GAVIN MARTIN
  Logotypes, 121
  Publications, 122–5, 127
  Stationery, business cards, folders, and forms, 124–7

MOUNT CARMEL HEALTH
  Advertising, 142–4, 147
  Building, office, and facilities graphics, 132, 134–9, 141
  Organizational brochures, 145, 149, 153
  Product sales literature, 151–2
  Promotional materials/sales aids, 142–5, 148–9, 150–3
  Publications, 146–8
  Signage, 134
  Vehicles, 140–1

PENNSTATE
  Building, office, and facilities graphics, 71
  Logotypes, 73
  Organizational brochures, 75
  Publications, 74–5
  Stationery, business cards, folders, and forms, 74

PILKINGTON
  Advertising, 104–7, 112
  Building, office, and facilities graphics, 109
  Corporate brochures, 107, 113–5
  Customized alphabets, 101
  Identity/design manuals, 100–1, 103, 106–7
  Logotypes, 101
  Product sales literature, 102–3
  Signage, 97–9
  Stationery, business cards, folders, and forms, 102, 108–9
  Vehicles, 110–1

PRUDENTIAL CORPORATION
  Advertising, 65
  Building, office, and facilities graphics, 57–9, 60
  Corporate brochures, 61, 63
  Identity/design manuals, 62
  Logotypes, 58
  Promotional materials/sales aids, 64–5
  Signage, 55, 60
  Stationery, business cards, folders, and forms, 62

Q8 — KUWAIT PETROLEUM INTERNATIONAL
  Building, office, and facilities graphics, 39, 40, 42, 46–9
  Identity/design manuals, 42–3
  Logotypes, 37
  Product packaging, 46
  Publications, 45
  Signage, 41
  Stationery, business cards, folders, and forms, 44–5
  Vehicles, 48

QUAKER STATE CORPORATION
  Advertising, 27, 33
  Customized alphabets, 31
  Identity/design manuals, 21–3
  Logotypes, 21
  Product packaging, 24, 26–7, 29, 30, 32
  Product sales literature, 25–6, 28, 31
  Promotional materials/sales aids, 25, 28, 32–3

Index III
Design Firms

Dixon & Parcels Associates, Inc.
New York, New York
- PennState, 68–77
- Quaker State Corporation, 18–33

Salvato & Coe
Columbus, Ohio
- Mount Carmel Health, 130–152

Wolff Olins
London, England
- Aston University, 78–91
- Gavin Martin, 118–127
- Pilkington, 94–115
- Prudential Corporation, 52–65
- Q8 — Kuwait Petroleum International, 34–49

for Corporate Design Directors . Advertising Executives . Graphic Designers . Marketing Executives . Commercial Artists . Corporate Identity Specialists

Corporate Design Systems 2

Nine Case Studies in Corporate Design Strategy

by Motoo Nakanishi and the CoCoMAS Committee

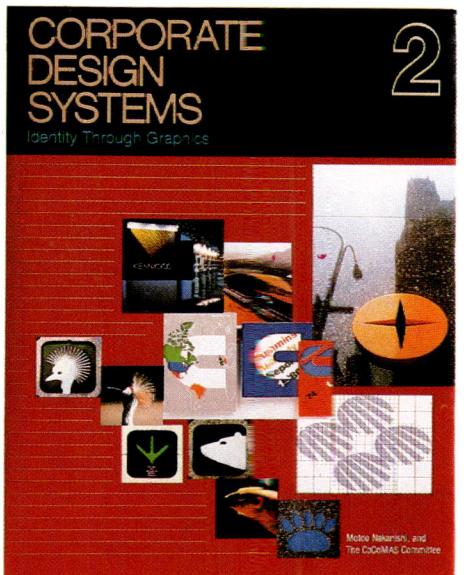

Anyone involved in creating graphics for business will find this collection a thought-provoking exploration of the possibilities of business graphics.

CORPORATE DESIGN SYSTEMS 2 shows in detail how designers for nine major corporations created new design identities for their clients. Included are:

CORPORATE DESIGN SYSTEMS 2
ISBN: 0-86636-004-2
Hardbound 9 x 12 in.
126 full-color pages
Over 325 full-color photographs

- Citibank, N.A. of New York, New York
- The P&O Group of Great Britain
- Watney, Mann, Truman Brewers, Ltd. of Great Britain
- Trio-Kenwood Corporation of Tokyo, Japan
- Cummins Engine Co. of Columbus, Indiana
- Clarks Ltd. of Somerset, England
- The Citizens National Bank of Seoul, Korea
- The National Zoological Park of the Smithsonian Institution, Washington, D.C.

Full-color photographs show the progression of a corporate identity program from conceptual sketches through finished materials.

  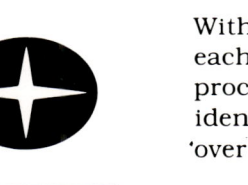

With an entire chapter devoted to each of these major projects, the process of creating a corporate identity is revealed step by step in 'over 325 full-color photographs of:

- Pre-existing corporate symbols
- Finished logos
- Signage
- Vehicle graphics
- Headquarters and retail location graphics
- Conceptual sketches
- Letterheads
- Printed matter
- Employee clothing
- Flags

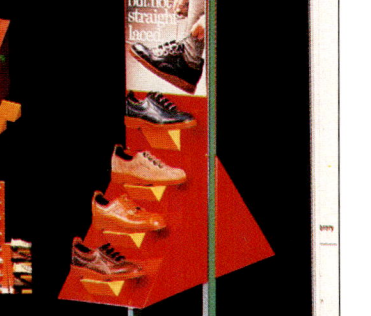

Informative text and captions describe the philosophy behind the designs, the design parameters, and how the various elements shown have been put into use.

Available at bookstores and art supply centers, and from the publisher, PBC International, Inc., One School Street, Glen Cove, New York 11542.